Sheepless Nights

Harriet

Also by Dinah Latham:

Walking Forward, Looking Back
A District Nurse's Life Journey

Sheepless Nights

Dinah Latham

ISBN: 9798671008265

PublishNation
www.publishnation.co.uk

This book is dedicated to the memory of
Jill Hardy
who always believed Harriet and I could learn to
sheep herd and who so loved my first book.

You left us too soon Jill…this one is for you

Preface

I entered retirement without much thought as to where it would lead other than to begin a journey into growing old. I had attended a couple of those pre-retirement sessions which appeared to address firstly financial issues and then fitness.

I remember leaving the meetings being fairly sure that I'd failed both assessments. Apparently, I should have been saving vast amounts from my income since the age of eighteen to stand any chance of managing independently on my pension should I be lucky enough to live longer than the three score years and ten.

I began to think this in itself appeared unlikely, as I had already begun reading the brightly coloured leaflet that awaited me on my seat when I arrived for the 'All about Retirement' session. The leaflet seemed to assume a level of fitness that was several degrees above mine with encouragement to continue the cycling, jogging, aerobics or twice weekly gym sessions as before I left employment.

I had spent many years working as a district nurse and midwife while, as a single parent, bringing up my four children, I wasn't sure where either savings for additional pensions or time for gym sessions was supposed to come from but I guess it clearly confirmed two things for me that I already knew. I was sure I would learn to manage on the pension I had... I'd grown used to managing on an inadequate income. Also, I have an aversion to headbands and leg warmers that shows no signs of diminishing should I find I do have time to exercise.

The positives were that I had recently downsized to my one bedroomed ground floor flat as the last of my children left home. It was an apartment without stairs (great for the arthritic knees) and had a very small garden that would allow me to fulfil a lifelong dream of owning a dog... hardly an outrageously unreasonable aspiration to hold.

Little did I know then where retirement, or my dog, would lead me or indeed any of the joy that I would discover as I journeyed into growing old in a society that sees all those of us who are retired as not only insignificant but burdensome.

They say life is what happens while waiting for something else. My retirement undoubtedly appeared to have an uncertain landscape as I crossed its threshold, so yes, I suppose I was waiting. This is my 'something else'.

Fifty Shades of Grey Hound

I was shaking as I walked to the post and suddenly it seemed to be a very long way away. My feet seemed tied to the ground and every footstep was a huge effort that didn't appear to be getting me any nearer the dreaded starting point. The strange eerie sound of the broadcaster's voice echoed out from the tannoy seeming to alert the whole county to mine and Harriet's presence on the trial field. I was distracted; Harriet was just not the right name for a sheepdog why on earth had I chosen such an unsuitable name for a working dog? We had been invited from our straw bale seat amongst the onlookers to take part, filling an unanticipated gap in the running order caused by a missing shepherd and his dog.

This was no ordinary trial. As I passed in front of the massive grandstand on my marathon trudge to the post, the words on the banners along the fence seemed to grow, each letter increasing in size with my every step… English National Sheepdog Trial. The three day yearly event has the leading competitors in the country taking part, all competing to qualify for a place in the International trial to be held later in the year.

The complete trial course is displayed in front of us; the enormity of the task right there for all to see. The sheep were released from the let out pen away at the top of the field. They were so far away it felt as though I was inspecting the scene through the wrong end of a telescope. I knew there were supposed to be five sheep but the number was indefinable due to the distance but more than that I appear to have lost the ability to count. I asked Harriet to look for sheep… if I can't see them, sure as 'eggs is eggs' she can't! I give her the come-bye command wondering whether she's going to make any attempt to even leave my side… when off she goes at a surprisingly rapid pace. I'm sure I hear an audible sudden intake of breath from every one of the thousand spectators as Harriet's outrun develops into a brilliantly choreographed manoeuvre… the like I've certainly never previously witnessed.

I fumble with my whistle to get her to stand behind the sheep, only to find I have no breath to blow it; my chest is so tight I feel as if I'm in a plaster jacket. The sheep are 'lifted' perfectly and steadily by Harriet (again a first) and I watch in amazement as she brings them, each and every one of them, through the 'fetch' gate down to my feet. I just manage to gain sufficient composure to direct her to move the sheep around me at the post … the plaster jacket refuses to allow me to turn round with her but I needn't have worried; the sheep walk around me with Harriet nudging them just enough to keep them on line, the lead sheep even seems to smile at me as she passes and they all head for the first drive gate.

I breathe possibly for the first time since we began. I just check to make sure this really is my dog as Harriet appears to be executing every part of this performance as though she really does deserve her place in this prestigious event and as though she's loaded with natural instinct. All five sheep go through the first drive gate and I blow a whistle note that I can't ever remember hearing before that encourages her to turn the sheep to begin the cross drive. My legs go to jelly as I allow what's left of my brain to determine that we're actually doing this; we really are following a straight line towards the final gate leaving two processes to complete… yes the most difficult bits, the 'shed' where we will need to divide the sheep before we can pen them and close the gate.

I begin to add together the marks we must have already been allocated by the judges in this impressive run, but I remember that I've lost my ability to count. I can visualize write-ups in the International Sheepdog Society magazine detailing the underdog who came good. All the sheep negotiate the final gate...

We turn the sheep with the tightest of turns round the gate and Harriet positions herself in exactly the best position behind sheep to begin the last part of the drive back to the shedding ring. This ring is clearly defined by carefully placed piles of sawdust on the outer edges of the large circle wherein I would need to divide my sheep prior to penning them.

Exactly at this point in the run, the sky suddenly darkens, storm clouds gather rapidly overhead. The rumbles of thunder begin to resonate around the course as the heavens open. I'm fighting to keep the sheep on line, I hastily reach over my head to grab and pull up my rain hood from around the back of my neck. So fierce was the onslaught that I yanked the peak down to prevent the rain from stinging my face. This last part of the drive seems to be going on forever; no drive has ever been this long. The sheep are beginning to string out... why has each of them got a different coloured collar on I wonder, and how come that smiley one in front has so many teeth, he has a top set as well, how did he manage that?

Every passing minute seems to intensify the elements of the flash storm, the wind, the lashing rain and the incessant thunder claps. As she moves on forward directly into the driving rain Harriet's eyes are merely slits. I call her round on the come-bye to keep the sheep in line for the shedding ring and her coat becomes parted to the skin as the wind flattens the long fur on her left side, I'm struggling to locate the shedding ring... never before have I been faced with such conditions anywhere let alone at a trial... hunting, searching, where is the ring, where the hell is the damn shedding ring? An abrupt streak of lightening illuminates something ahead of me as I dare to leave the post in my search; it looks circular, it has to be the shedding ring but it's so far away and it's black, pitch black. As I edge nervously forward, I turn towards Harriet commanding her to stop; she drops flat to her belly, a wet bedraggled example of her former self. Where are the sheep, I can't see any sheep!?

I continue moving forward, towards the blackened ring. I can't seem to reach it, I try to quicken my pace, my heart pounding and my mind turning somersaults. As suddenly as it started, the rain stops, but the wind continues to whine. As I reach the dark hole appearing before me, I find myself on a cliff edge and I'm peering over to see a large ram with huge horns perched on a craggy ledge some twenty feet below me.

A bell rings loudly over the tannoy timing me out … the trial is over, we've failed to complete the course. With a sense of relief, I turn ….reaching out to turn off my alarm clock. Harriet's wet nose finds my hand as I grope to locate the switch. I'm still struggling to breath easily when her whine in my ear tells me just how near she is. She's laid flat across my chest wanting to be near me. But I can still hear rain. In my half-awake state I'm pleased to discover she's not soaking wet. She has never liked storms, and heavy rain is hitting the windows; a distant rather gentle rumble of thunder allows me to reassure her that the worst is now over…. I think about the wet muddy walk that surely awaits us as a murky dawn begins to break.

Where has this retired life led me that I could have such a detailed dream about a subject that was so far from anything I had ever encountered in my former working life? Previously I would have known no more about sheep than to smile at the quintessentially English picture postcard image of springtime in the country. The link to what is now so much a part of my life, is Harriet.

* * *

I always had a liking for 'One Man and his Dog' and joined with many in regretting its disappearance from our screens. I'm not sure why particularly… yes it was reminiscent of what many of us believed to be true rural life with something reassuringly everlasting about its weekly constancy on BBC 2 night viewing for some 20 years. So much so that it really should have been no surprise that its demise caused such a public rumpus when the 'powers that be' decided it was time to 'pull the plug' in the late 90s.

Then I had no idea quite how involved I was destined to become in this country pursuit when retirement arrived on my doormat. Well, strictly speaking it was Harriet, the rescue Bearded Collie puppy who literally landed on the mat, all four paws looking too big for her black and white paint-splogged body… two big brown eyes staring enquiringly with her head tipped sideways squashing her left ear. Her coat grew rapidly longer and shaggier, seeming to change colour every week until she became a tousled mass of fur in shades of grey from nearly black through dark charcoal to bits that try hard to be white or, more accurately, bits that struggle to *stay* white.

I instantly warmed to her as a companion who has even less control over her hair than me, her owner, and frequently looks as though she's come through a hedge backwards, even when she hasn't… although on most occasions I manage to stay a little less grubby than she does.

The daily walks began, new experiences for us both, exploring local footpaths that have always been here but hitherto largely untrodden by me… one of the joys of retirement, time to wander. Mind you 'wander' isn't a word I'd attach to Harriet's explorations; hers is more like one of those supermarket rush-arounds where you dash up and down each aisle grabbing as much as possible for your trolley in the shortest amount of time… only in her case there's no gathering, just sniffing and peeing.

It was on these walks that Harriet began to show sufficient interest in sheep for me to become concerned. I'm not sure exactly what I was apprehensive about, but seeing her staring through fences, seemingly fascinated by grazing sheep, made me uneasy. I was someone who knew very little about dogs (Harriet is the first dog I've ever had) and clearly I knew absolutely nothing about sheep… what might happen if she were off lead?

The prospect troubled me, after all I had heard tell of dogs who risked being shot because they chased sheep. Was Harriet a sheep chaser, just waiting to be let loose? Other dog walkers I met and walked with had an assortment of breeds of mutt although Labradoodles seemed to outnumber all other varieties two to one! These are woolly creatures who don't shed their coat I'm told and are therefore prized possessions for the population of the Southeast who seemingly are allergic to all other dogs! I'd always thought a Labradoodle was a crossbreed but then what do I know? They don't stare at sheep that's for sure. Early on in my dog-walking career, I did meet one Border Collie owner who I attempted to engage in conversation hoping she would give me advice on how to overcome the sheep gazing. She was very confused, telling me her collie was addicted to chasing tyres!

I decided to try and find someone who could answer questions for me about sheep dogs and sheep.

It took me sometime but I found a couple, Pam and Gordon, with 40 sheep about half an hour away from me, who invited me over to see how Harriet behaved in the presence of sheep. I'm not quite sure what I expected but my hope was that they would be able to explain her reactions and how I might be able to manage her off the lead if she approached sheep.

At first glance when she (and I) were put in a pen with half a dozen large sheep, I was surprised to find she was somewhat nervous of these large woolly creatures as they stamped their feet at her and drove her against the bars while doing their best to push me over at the same time. I was quite relieved when the farmer's wife suggested we came out of the pen and joined her in a cup of tea from her flask. Harriet went immediately under my car which I'd parked alongside the hedge in the field; clearly she had not enjoyed her first experience close to sheep. I chatted to Pam, expressing my worries about how I would manage her on our walks should we come across a field of sheep with her running free. She was just explaining to me the possibility of turning a dog off sheep when the farmer came out through a gate about 200yds away at the very top of the field with all the sheep flooding through after him as he attempted to move them all to another field. At this moment Harriet darted out from under the car, streaked up the field barking loudly and proceeded to take all the sheep back into the field they'd just left… all too fast, all too close, chasing as fast as she could!

With Gordon, the farmer, shouting at me to get my dog under control, I ran after Harriet imploring her to lie down. As I reached the top of the field I turned to the left where I had seen Harriet disappear through the gateway chasing the sheep back into the field from whence they came. I could now see her rounding up the sheep and bringing the terrified flock tearing towards me… looking to me as their only chance of rescue from this marauding dog. Momentarily, I considered flight as my only escape from death by cloven hooves but when I forced my eyes open I was surrounded by heavily breathing sheep with a panting dog following on, seemingly decidedly confused, staring at me as if to say "Hello what are you doing here?". It was as though she had been in her own little world, unaware of anything but sheep. Finally, with my pounding heart still in my mouth, I was able to push my way through the puffing sheep, attach her lead and bring her out through the gate to be greeted by Pam explaining that it was her natural instinct that had made her take off after them when they were moving.

"It would be a real shame not to use that instinct" Pam said, adding "Why don't you learn to teach her to work sheep?" My somewhat cynical response was to remind her that I didn't actually have any sheep! To me this was surely a fairly fundamental flaw in her plan. This statement of fact was dismissed out-of-hand by Pam with an equally disparaging comment "Well why does that matter, come here next Thursday and learn!"

* * *

There was something in her tone and manner that reminded me of an episode in my previous working life. The district nursing superintendent who accepted me for district nurse training in London some forty years ago was equally unimpressed when I announced that I couldn't ride a bike and couldn't read a map. "You'll learn" was her retort..." Here's your list of patients to be visited tomorrow. Pick your bike up from the yard in the morning!"

* * *

Standing in the middle of the sheep Pam said "Come here on Thursday, bring your wellingtons and wear something warm; it's going to be wet and cold next week."

What I didn't tell her was that I live in a one bedroom pint-sized flat with hardly a garden to speak of... just a table-top sized patio; neither did I divulge my limited experience with dogs which I thought might just be a handicap.

I drove away from this first encounter with sheep feeling stunned, wondering how I'd suddenly allowed myself to become a doubtful cast member in an obscure drama about which I knew absolutely nothing and the only attribute I had to recommend me for the part was a pair of wellington boots.

Recounting this now, maybe a subtitle for the book should have been...

'Learning to sheep herd when you don't have any sheep!'

However, this was how it all began. I actually, at this point, believed I was doing this because my dog might like it but, surprisingly, it didn't take long for me to become captivated by what Harriet and I were trying to do. It crept up on me unexpectedly. Having thought I was doing this to exercise my dog using her natural instincts, I found it was me who wanted to learn, understand and do more.

* * *

I'm reminded of me as a pre teenager obsessed with reading the Sue Barton nursing stories ... desperate to finish each one, to return it to the library and collect the next one in the series. I think it was these books that sowed the seed of my determination to train as a nurse. I really believed then that I would lay my hands on fevered brows and patients would heal.... encouraged next by Emergency Ward 10 where I think the number of young handsome doctors forever accompanying every student nurse in her industrious bed making chores, spurred on the longing to serve.

In my day, when nursing was considered to be a 'vocation', it was thought that, once nursing was in your blood, you never really recovered... it was like one of those infections that can be treated and made to lie dormant but will, when conditions are temperate, rise up and demand attention; like an addiction that had to be satisfied, a thirst that had to be satiated.

* * *

I now found myself purchasing films made by well-known triallists, I read every book I could find about learning to train a sheepdog. I became enthusiastic and convinced this was the way to go... and dispirited in equal measure to find that each and every command issued by the instructor didn't, when I repeated it, result in the perfect execution of the outrun or fetch when we next went to the sheep. I tried relentlessly to replicate what I'd seen or read but clearly Harriet didn't study either the film or book with the same level of concentration and commitment that I did.

Here I am now, addicted to sheepherding, unable to wait to get out on the field. On mornings when I'm going training, I wake and feel a buzz of excitement like a kid who realises as his eyes open that today is his birthday. How ridiculous is that... retired, bordering on being labelled 'elderly', with the wrong type of dog and no sheep!

When I say the wrong type of dog, that's not strictly true. By far the majority of working sheep dogs now are Border Collies. The *Bearded* Collie was used historically on hill farms to bring the sheep down for lambing or shearing. The breed originated in Scotland. Legend has it that a Polish merchant traded a shipment of grain for sheep there and brought his Polish Lowland sheepdogs to move his purchase. It is said that the Scottish farmer was so impressed with the herding ability of these dogs that he traded several sheep for several of his dogs and these Polish dogs were bred with local Scottish sheepdogs to produce the Bearded Collie.

The Bearded Collie was used particularly to bring large numbers of sheep down from the hills; being used at a time when sheep were driven, oft times many miles, taking sheep to market. They were known as droving dogs, working with their farmer master by their side. They have a reputation as a companion dog and could be seen in days of yore at the end of a long droving day, in the local public house after the market, resting at the feet of their master.

But they have largely been replaced by the faster, sleeker Border Collie. The Beardie has a slower more loping gait, generally moving at a steadier pace. When compared to the Border Collie on the trial field the differences in style are evident. Many seasoned farmers and triallers I have met speak as though the Border Collie has superseded the Beardie. As you might expect, I disagree and am very defensive in any discussion that voices such an evident truth!

From Pillock to Post

So, somewhat unexpectedly, I found myself with Pam and her sheep trying to follow her instructions while standing in a field with the rain coming down like 'stair rods' being battered by gale force winds, struggling to stay upright with rain dripping down my neck and somehow seeping into my boots with me wondering what on earth I had let myself in for. Harriet was similarly bedraggled, looking very skinny with her long wet hair clinging close to her body, with rain running down her face and nose from her fringe plastered down over her eyes. Underneath all of that she was alert ready for action staring steadfastly ahead at the sheep, seemingly transfixed, certainly totally unperturbed by the weather.

This was a picture to be repeated many times over the following days, weeks and months as we continued with as many lessons as possible. I began to realise just what a lengthy journey this learning to sheep herd was going to be for both of us, Harriet as well as me. But rain or shine Harriet and I were there, making the absolute most of any time and training we could find.

I used to reflect sometimes on just how easy it all looked on 'One Man and his dog... the 'One Man' always standing confidently at the post, the dog obediently responding to each and every one of his whistles, the sheep moving steadily. It always looked so effortless... such a peaceful country scene. I had no idea then of just how physically and mentally exhausting that ten minutes at the post was for him... I always thought the dog worked hard, and didn't really get enough of the credit when that gate swung closed on the sheep and the applause echoed around the ground.

To begin with there is an awful lot more running around the field or the pen trying to stop your dog either crashing through the middle of the sheep as they flock closely together or alternatively trying to stop him circling the sheep; to keep him behind the sheep going both right (aaway) or left (come bye). So much chasing around in those early days it was absolute heaven to sink into a bath on my return home... *very reminiscent of my early days in nursing on the ward, soaking tired feet at the end of a long day!*

As we practised and re-practised each and every one of those manoeuvres, I could never believe just how much attention was involved. Whenever we had managed to execute an acceptable outrun and Harriet had picked up (lifted) a packet of sheep and was bringing them (the fetch) down to me, my brain was sending loads of messages that I was supposed to see, focus on, respond to... the sheep are coming too fast, should I stop her? Where are the sheep facing? Which way do I need to flank (send) her to get the sheep to travel in a straight line, to get all the sheep through that gate? Where IS the gate? Where ARE the sheep? Even when we had advanced far enough in the training for me to be able to more or less stand still and not have to run after her everywhere trying to get her in the right position... even then I always seemed to finish every exercise facing the wrong way and out of breath simply because, with all that brain stuff trying to get through, I would hold my breath until I was in danger of collapsing through lack of oxygen. I was supposed to find sufficient breath throughout to blow the whistle, with a mouth so so dry. The strange thing is that while everything seems to be happening so fast, there's another sense in which it's the longest 10 minutes ever; probably it's the amount of concentration that stretches the time.

I believe it is said that it takes about two years to train a dog for trialling. What it took me a considerable time to process was of course that maybe so for a *farm* dog; a dog who is working sheep on probably a daily basis, who is learning with his master and able to repeat all those intricate trial manoeuvres many times. Without sheep of our own… and perhaps only access and lessons with sheep possibly once a week, progress is inevitably a lot slower. Another old farmer told me he believed you needed one year for every leg of a dog before he or she was really trained, ie four years.

We did begin to enter a few very small trials with cradle and nursery levels of competition. I'm not even sure 'competition' was in it for me …. it was about me just being able to see what trialling was all about and what we were both capable of. When I look back on those very early experiences, I'm embarrassed to say that it was also about gaining access to sheep for me… to go to a different field other than my weekly outing to Pam's… to work with different sheep and try desperately to perhaps understand, even if it proved impossible for me to appreciate, what this 'sheep-sense' was all about.

The first few were chaotic, both Harriet and I with next to no confidence, her over excited, me over anxious… not a good combination. Not very many runners and therefore possible spectators, but I swear every one of them at my first ever trial lined the fence to 'watch the Beardie run'. I was to learn that this was unfortunately quite a common occurrence as it seems very few Beardies trial, it has been known but I've not met any yet. Being something of a spectacle when walking to the post does nothing for my nerves. But even so the constant support and encouragement offered by many of these great people at the Kent farm trials has been such a help.

Happily, this spectator interest has waned somewhat because we're both not really very good and clearly don't show sufficient promise on the field to hold much attention. I sometimes hear mutterings behind me as I walk on to the trial field now where one well known competitor will be saying to another "See that woman over there... do you know she lives in a flat, she's got no sheep, not even a garden and the wrong sort of dog and guess what, it's called Harriet... what sort of name is that for anything that works sheep?"

My first ever attempt only had 4 sheep at each let out (rather than the more usual 5)... but it was the right number for what Harriet was about to do with them. I wasn't expecting much... "Just outrun lift and fetch them to me Harriet, please my luv just this once". Outrun not too bad, too close at the top behind the sheep to effect a decent lift... then came the disastrous four barks, scattering sheep, one sheep in each of the 4 corners of the trial field with me calling Harriet back to my feet and her looking up at me as if to say "Will that do?" This was the first of many trials when I would turn and signal to the judge that we were retiring. Etiquette requires that you and your dog gather your sheep and drive them to the exhaust pen after your run (a pen holding all the sheep as they finish each run)... in this case 'the walk of shame'. This time I actually had to call for help to gather and remove our sheep from the course, I didn't want to tempt a repeat performance of the barking scatter! As we left the field, I'd like to say with tail between our legs but Harriet doesn't understand the meaning of that phrase; it was me who was trying to slink away... Harriet trotted along nonchalantly looking up at me as if to say "Well it was hardly worth bothering with those few was it?"

One of the seasoned triallers put his hand on my shoulder saying "The first thousand trials are the worst luv... keep going, we're supposed to enjoy this you know!"

I wouldn't want any reader to run away with the idea that I don't understand that the sheep at every trial are some farmer's livelihood and this sort of behaviour is not acceptable on any trial field, even a first attempt. It's not an escapade I'm proud of and nothing has been that bad since.

I did go to the organiser of the trial to apologise after Harriet's performance and he had with him the farmer who owned the sheep. He was kind enough to tell me that part of the problem was that he didn't think his sheep had ever seen a Beardie before and he felt that had played a part in the sheep flying off. In fact he encouraged me to keep on trying; real kindness.

These are training trials usually running through the winter months where hopeful triallists take their young dogs to try them out on either cradle, nursery or novice trials. They are usually set up on a smaller field with a limited size course without too many obstacles to encourage, but not over-face, young dogs. These allow us to work at learning the art of the trial… not simply by what we are able to accomplish (or not!) on the field, but by watching experienced handlers and if we're lucky getting tips from many 'old hands' on every aspect from setting the dog up before the outrun to why you missed that gate with the sheep.

It was on this field that I did manage to complete my first nursery trial; a really small beginners' trial but we actually penned our sheep. I think we only managed all the sheep through one of the gates and there was no way any on-looker would have proclaimed it demonstrated a future national partnership, but we did it; Harriet and I had at last completed our trial to a round of applause… me so overcome that I forgot to let the sheep out of the pen and had to be reminded to escort them with Harriet driving them to the exhaust pen to recover. I wanted to pick her up in my arms and hug her forever! Instead I simply ruffled the fur on the top of her head and she skipped around my feet all the way off the field in a somewhat undignified non-sheepdog way with her big brown eyes staring up at me full of pleasure because she had got it right for me. We were not placed, we were definitely not in line for a rosette on that occasion but I cannot remember being so delighted with any achievement since I opened the envelope to discover I had passed my finals and was now a state registered nurse. In fact this kindly sheepdog society awarded me a framed picture one year, a photo of Harriet and me working the sheep. The inscription underneath said 'To Dinah and Harriet awarded for Perseverance! This sport is called trialling for a reason...

As a bonus trials all start early, very early. Five thirty seems to be the time I have to set my alarm clock to get to any of them. I guess as trialling has originated from farming stock, 'early to rise' has been the maxim that most farmers live by so it has grown up as a tradition that 7.30 am on the field for the first run seems obligatory.

I remain forever grateful for every bit of help from so many people while I'm learning. It's dispiriting at times to realise I will never reach the heights of those, much more important, open trials. Sheep-sense is a skill I haven't got but that all farmers, and most seasoned triallists, don't even realise they've got and yet they demonstrate it at every run. Being brought up in the farming world, as so many of them have been, they have soaked up through their skin more knowledge and ability about sheep behaviour than I can ever hope to own. Coming in at a late age with a less than the ideal breed of dog for the task (I wouldn't change her for the world!) and no sheep to practise on day in and day out, we are at a huge disadvantage Harriet and me... but such a rich well of experience to tap into at every turn.

The disadvantage of 'no-sheep-to-practise-on' was to be a recurring theme throughout my whole sheepherding journey that effected every aspect of our learning at every stage and was to return frequently to haunt me.

Recently, eavesdropping near the 'let out' pen (the pen that holds the sheep before they are let out five at a time for each run) at a trial I overheard an experienced sheep and dog handler put forward the view that really the sport of sheepdog trialling shouldn't be available to anyone who didn't own their own sheep. Without owning sheep to practise on, he felt they were destined to always be inexperienced and therefore ended up hassling sheep at nursery trials, 'chasing' what is a farmer's livelihood.

I've run that through in my mind many times and have found myself wondering whether he's right. It is a sport that is meant to reflect the everyday work the farmer does with his dog; a task it's unlikely will ever be part of Harriet's and my daily work.

The trial course is designed to replicate the everyday challenges that the working sheepdog tackles but set up in a format to make it into a competition... so most courses are set up following a similar layout. The objective is to send your dog to collect the five sheep set up at a point usually more than 250yards away. The handler must remain at the post while the dog then 'lifts' the sheep in a calm orderly manner, (wish I could teach Harriet the meaning of the words calm and orderly). The dog then drives or guides those sheep down through the 'fetch' gate to the handler before undertaking a triangular course driving the sheep through two further sets of gates and into the shedding ring, depicted in sawdust, in front of the handler. The handler then leaves the post, enters the ring and assists the dog in separating two sheep from the rest and holding them apart until the judge indicates the 'shed' as accepted.

Finally, the sheep are encouraged, or more accurately persuaded into a small pen against their will and the handler closes the gate. Each section of the trial is allocated a number of points totalling a hundred in all. Points are deducted from every section according to how well each part has been executed. The winner is the handler who completes the course within the time limit and has accumulated the highest number of points.

Historically these trials were only used by farmers, where each farmer set out to prove he had the best, most capable dog when working sheep. Only much later was it really developed into a sport. The first ever recorded trial in the United Kingdom was held in Wales in 1873 with 10 dogs competing. Trials quickly spread to England and Scotland and today the sport continues to be popular throughout the world. When it comes to trialling, the Border Collie is by far the most popular breed of dog used... actually it's rare to see any other breed of dog used even for farm work. They have been bred specifically for the task for many years now and who was bred by whom and out of which bitch and dog, who's certificated and how long the breeding line is, seems to be a subject for many a conversation amongst spectators at any trial.

For the uninitiated, Harriet is associated with nothing and no-one... she was a rescue puppy and the only certificate she is ever likely to possess is one that I might just give her for managing her first full length of a special doggie therapeutic swimming pool! I'll put it in the file with mine where it will probably be as unlikely to herald the start of a blisteringly successful swimming career, as was mine.

* * *

My father wanted me to swim the channel when I grew up and so, in preparation, he had me swimming the width of the lake at Black Park in Iver on freezing cold Sunday mornings when I was nine years old. Anyone who knows it will agree, it's definitely a big lake!

* * *

Juxtaposed with this opinion, 'only-sheep-owners-should-be-trialling' there are some well-known triallers who believe that unless the non-farmers amongst us are encouraged to learn and partake in the sport, it could be in danger of becoming extinct. There are many farms with sheep now where the quad bike is more visible than any sheep dog of any breed. I suppose you could say that where the tractor has taken over from the horse the quad bike has taken over from the sheepdog. Yes, it's possible to hurtle around a field on a quad bike and get all the sheep to flock together and even run in vaguely the right direction but no quad bike can shed off the one limping sheep you want to look at or guide a certain number off down the run or into a pen. Even less can you position a quad bike to help a ewe who's struggling to lamb, whereas a dog not only sheds her off but holds her there to allow the shepherd to assist with the birthing.

I have tried watching quad bike sheep farming but it's a really noisy, soulless operation and it in no way compares with watching the experienced master and sheepdog working calmly and steadily together to achieve a herding task. The beauty of the task is nothing short of breath taking.

My breath is often taken when Harriet and I are working together, but for much less auspicious happenings...

Who was it who said "you can kick a quad bike but you can talk to a dog?"

I feel I need to accept the reality that Harriet and I belong to, or are trying very hard to join, a rather strange group of people known as hobby or weekend triallists. We are a motley crew that on the face of it don't quite fit in anywhere, a random group of strange people, some of us inner city dwellers, who have somehow become addicted to 'one man and his dog' stuff; there are some of our group who do have access to sheep even though they don't own any themselves.

When I travel to trials on different farms, even when I'm not competing, it becomes clear that many of us hobby triallists are clearly pet owners at heart, while it is evident that the farm dog is definitely seen as a tool. Someone once passed comment that clearly many a farmer thinks more of his tractor than his dog. I think I can almost comprehend that, even though surely his dog, as a living breathing animal, must be more of a companion while working than the tractor?

But as an onlooker, I find it hard to understand, what I'm only able to describe as, the poor conditions in which some farmers keep their dogs. While I've expected these dogs to be kept outside and not sleeping on the sofa like Harriet, I have found it hard to fathom keeping them in often dark, makeshift kennels with little or no bedding, repeatedly chained for long periods. It can seem harsh when the only attention the dogs receive is when they are released and expected to work stock.

Not all farmers manage their dogs this way by any means and I've seen many farmers and triallists who administer to all their loyal worker dogs in a very considered respectful way; taking them out for free time exercise, ensuring they're well fed... they just fall short at the suggestion of sharing their breakfast toast crusts with their friend.

Sheepdog Training Clinics

There came a time when Harriet and I were fortunate enough to have the opportunity to go to some sheepdog training clinics. I was vaguely concerned by the word 'clinic' but was reassured that it didn't involve taking any clothes off, which would certainly have played a part in any 'clinic' I'd ever previously encountered. The opposite was true here, these clinics very often involved increasing the number of layers you wore to cope with the icy blasts of wind, rain, hail and anything else not even mentioned in the weather forecast.

One of our most experienced triallists gave of his time and expertise at a farm to help others like me struggling to take part in this working sheepdog world.

It was a surprise to me to find anyone seriously into sheepdog training was even interested in helping the likes of me.

Of course we didn't need to be in this new domain for long before some of the major differences were very evident; differences between 'us' and 'them' of the farming fraternity. There were other sheepdog owners among us who did have access to sheep on a daily basis, who were working shepherds wanting help from experts on refining their dogs in the tasks required for the trial field or to ask for help with a particular problem they were having with their dog when working sheep. For instance some of the dogs were inclined to grip the sheep while others could be too timid when ewes stood to the dog. Our trainer would assist the farmer in managing any problems.

I was to learn that these very special people who offer us the opportunity of taking our dogs to these clinics, have a real interest in keeping the art of sheepdog trialling going. Here, those who fear the demise of the sheepdog trial encourage us hobby, weekend triallists to take a live interest in the sport.

Once we had the basics of what sheepherding was all about, and Harriet was able to flank and follow basic commands, these workshops became our lifeline to learning more about every aspect of the shepherding world. Not only did it give us access to bigger numbers of sheep, but they afforded each of us the opportunity to learn from watching each other. Watching other handlers and their dogs being advised and corrected meant that I learned and benefitted from every session over the 2 or 3 day course even when I've been simply leaning on the fence watching how others were improving. I was then returning to the field for perhaps my second personal session of the day with so much more education than merely my first attempt in my pocket. If only Harriet would learn as much watching other dogs working, we might be heading for the national trials by now!

Sadly, that isn't exactly the way it usually plays out. I advance for my second go, with determination and a bucket full of hope, and am leaving wondering why it went wrong this time. However, the support and inspiration received from these sessions can't always be measured in brilliance. I usually leave in awe of my trainer's expertise and the time he's prepared to give to minions like Harriet and I.

Going to these clinics has become really important to both of us not only for all we take away with us to try to put into practise ready for next time but also for the reinforcement to keep going… when we have shown so little promise. These clinics have been much needed precious haven-days.

Frequently, the tension that exists with all the hard work is broken with bouts of laughter that keep us all coming back for more… very often caused by something one of us is trying to get right but sometimes it's the dog that causes the hilarity by either disappearing off with the sheep and failing to return or, as Harriet did recently, set off downhill and across two large fields as directed by me. She was following my direction but was still some 300yds away from the sheep I'd asked her to collect when, midway, she saw what she thought was a much closer group of sheep in the corner of an adjacent field. This corner group was still some distance away but nearer than the flock I'd sent her for. Everyone watched as Harriet changed her direction and headed off to this closer group. It was then she discovered they weren't sheep at all in this handier corner, but simply a stack of white boxes! Even though I was too far away to see the expression on her face, I swear she was embarrassed by her mistake.

This display was 'caught on camera'. These clinics offer all of us so much; we have other experienced sheepdog handlers who support our trainer and between them they record our performances, both good and bad and display the films while we munch our packed lunch in the barn. This gives us all a chance to critique our own efforts being able to actually see the mistakes 'live' with the training team encouraging us to see where and how to improve.

Then of course there's always the times when you land in the mud as the sheep take your legs out from underneath you as your over enthusiastic dog fails to react to your stop command. These are the times when I've been 'caught on camera' and wonder why on earth I got involved in this game and didn't take up crochet or cake making in retirement.

To watch our trainer assess every new dog and owner as they advance on to the field is awe inspiring; to see the respect given to him by every dog as he attempts to help each and every dog and owner with so many different training problems is an education in itself. I avidly seek the why and how of every action he undertakes in my desire to take in and soak up any and everything he is willing to share... such a generous gift to all of us.

It was here that I learned the difference in the way the Border Collie and the Bearded Collie work... all the dogs I've seen have been Border or Border-Cross dogs. So before understanding the different ways they work I was always comparing Harriet's lack of speed and expertise with that of the Border Collie.

I had become used to trainers who really understood very little about the specific differences in the way the Beardie works on sheep. Working with Harriet became so much more satisfying when I understood the working history of her breed, when I could appreciate not just her limitations but some of the instincts coming through from her genes.

I only fully understood that difference when the trainer demonstrated Harriet's abilities on larger groups of sheep moving and driving them. It was then I began to understand the difference in her breeding; differences in style aligned to her heritage.

The trainer once said to me:

"Remember not to compare Harriet's performance with that of the Border Collie. She is not, and never will be a Border. She's not a Lamborghini - she's a Land Rover... and Land Rovers are very useful on a farm!"

I now have this emblazoned on my fridge... and while we'll never be able to compete at any of the big national sheepdog competitions, (almost as unlikely is the prospect of me ever owning a Land Rover), the comment helps keep me real... and why the heck would anyone choose a Lamborghini over a Land Rover anyway!!

I haven't always found it easy not to compare her with others and, even more to the point, my own shortcomings sometimes shine out like a beacon alongside other participants at the clinic, particularly when they are 'old hands' at understanding this elusive sheep behaviour.

On one of these clinics we had set up a trial where we could learn the whys and the wherefores of the trial and the etiquette involved in trialling.

I sent Harriet on an outrun slightly downhill where the five sheep had been pushed off line when they saw Harriet advancing and had congregated over to the right hand side. She 'lifted' not too badly and proceeded to 'fetch' them really quite well up the incline to me at a steady pace. I was beginning to feel quite pleased with her and wondered if anyone watching would be similarly impressed. Then as the sheep were coming forward with Harriet well off at the back, one of them suddenly went down; just laid down flat on the ground with its head between its hooves. I knew this sometimes happened, a sheep would refuse to take part, but it was usually when the dog was applying too much pressure and hassling the group too much. I was surprised because I hadn't felt Harriet had done that. Nevertheless, I knew that the right thing to do next was to gather the rest of the sheep and get Harriet to return them to the one who had opted out of the game when he would get up and re-join the pack. I had learned that you never sent your dog to take the one stray sheep to the group; it was always the group that needed to be taken to the one. We managed that and again I was quite pleased that it seemed to be going okay, but the solo sheep didn't get up and join the crowd as I expected. I abandoned the trial knowing that now once we had regathered the sheep together I needed to go nearer the action to work together with Harriet so we could carefully drive the group off the field to the exhaust pen.

I had to get Harriet to re gather the sheep from a wider area this time, they had gone off in several directions. We had to work harder, me with my commands and directions, Harriet to bring them farther back up the field to the one sheep who seemed determined not to play today. As I went deeper into the field in my attempt to help Harriet, out of the corner of my eye, I saw the judge, clip board in hand advancing towards me and behind him I heard the trundle of a tractor and turned to see it traveling up with its bucket raised on the front. The judge very quietly asked me to call Harriet off. I was utterly confused, at a loss to understand what I'd done. My head was spinning "What on earth was happening, surely that was right 'taking the many to the few?" I continued 'the walk of shame' off the field with the judge.

I was shocked to learn that the poor sheep was dead; he'd collapsed and died and I was trying to make him stand and join the crowd.

I was later assured that it was nothing to do with Harriet... she had not treated the sheep badly or gripped or anything awful, it was simply an elderly sheep who'd had enough. I still wonder if I'd been out there alone how many times would I have attempted to re-gather that poor sheep! The farmer and several other course members were reassuring and those who regularly worked with sheep smiled that I was a bit taken aback (thank goodness that one wasn't caught on film, it might have been used as a lesson in 'how not to...' for years.)

They weren't the least bit shocked and had no interest in why or what had happened. To them it was an everyday event it seemed. Apparently sheep are well known for dropping dead when it's least expected and when there's no definitive reason.

* * *

Death was very much part of my life before retirement working as a district nurse when, particularly through the later years of my career I was a palliative care specialist caring for patients and families choosing to manage the last months of their lives at home.

* * *

So while I was no stranger to death or even sudden death, it took some adjusting to adapt to the cursory attention given in farming life to the death of an animal and I was somewhat disturbed by how much animal deaths saddened me... a reaction that continues to stay with me now whenever I'm involved with farm work. It's something to do with finding it difficult to think of something dying out there in the field alone apparently with no-one on hand to care.

Yet, I recognise that I'm at ease with eating mutton rather than lamb, primarily because the sheep has led a full life as intended by the time it gets to my plate; munching, wandering, ruminating following the natural order of things... so of course what should follow is for the sheep to be 'at home' in the field when he breathes his last; and to avoid a live trip to the abattoir must surely be a plus.

I might have been an OK partner for a GP (general practitioner), but I'd have been useless as a farmer's wife. Actually that applies in more ways than one... all that catering, huge home cooked meals with the smell of home baked bread would never have emanated from any kitchen I played a part in. That's probably an out of date vision of rural domesticity... but the 'keep warm' oven in the range would be more likely to have a vulnerable baby lamb resting in it than a mutton casserole if I were there.

I always try to keep a diary of notes I make after each clinic, detailing all I've learned and adding comments made on our performance, trying to maximise every bit of tuition I've been offered. On my journey home from the clinic and the trial, I'm assembling thoughts in my head to record when I get back.

As I was getting out of my car with my wellington boots and the rest of my gear.

I thought back to my sheep... I didn't actually even suspect the poor thing might have died but maybe our brains can't make sense of things when we're busy determinedly focusing on what we believe is happening; I believed my sheep was playing dead something I had learnt about... not dropping dead. Whenever I now see a tractor with a bucket, I see my sheep being unceremoniously scooped from the field ..... will I ever learn enough about sheep?

As I heard a farmer say recently at a trial when something similar had happened "Well you know what they say mate, buy a sheep, buy a shovel!"

A Lost Opportunity

Harriet travels on the back seat of my car... she comes everywhere with me and I rarely leave her at home. It was always my desire as a district nurse/ midwife to have a dog on the back seat, as many country district nurses did in the 1950s and 60s. I was unable to manage it then but have had Harriet there ever since I retired. While there is no problem with leaving her, I choose not to on most occasions. I think I've unknowingly trained her to fit in with so many areas of my life because it suits me to have her with me.

Harriet is first and foremost a pet, her essential role is that of companion. This goes back to the original droving role historically undertaken by the Bearded Collie when she would have driven sheep to market with her shepherd, alongside her. I love watching her when we are lucky enough to be given the opportunity to drive big numbers of sheep from one field to another. To see her drop in behind a flock of sheep, watching them all turn; to see her head down, perfect style, concentration on the task in hand... absolutely loving it. Watching her doing what she believes she was made for is indeed a unique pleasure.

One evening I was in my car and turned a sharp corner to find myself almost surrounded by sheep all over the road, all it seemed facing in different directions. I then saw the rather harassed farmer struggling without a dog to move about 60 sheep along the road. I wound down the window saying I had a sheepdog in my car, asking if he'd like some help. The farmer really looked interested, "Not arf" came the hasty reply... I leapt out of the car excited on Harriet's behalf, thinking how great it was going to be to let her be useful; driving was the one thing I knew she could do... "I'll drop her here at the back of the pack" I called.

I opened the back door of the car before realising... I'd left her at home...

I turned back towards the farmer and his sheep, stuttering my apology feeling totally ridiculous, stumbling hastily back into my car. My embarrassment was further compounded when I realised I had my whistle round my neck... I was making one of my very few trips without her which is when I take advantage of her absence to practise my whistle commands!

I still turn a rosy shade of pink when I picture the farmer relating to his family how he had come across an escapee from an elderly care home who believed she had an imaginary sheepdog in her car. I comfort myself when I look back on this event with the laughs he must have had, at my expense, relating the story in the pub.

I sidled off quickly regretting the missed opportunity not only for Harriet but for me to perhaps make a connection with a farmer and his sheep which could possibly have resulted in being able to attend his farm on occasion and help.

I drive on sifting through other missed opportunities in my life and am quite heartened to realise how few there are and even more pleased to find that there are even less regrets. On the whole, life has been good to me... or so it feels today. Would I have preferred a career as a shepherdess? The idyllic vision of a cottage situated in the corner of a large field where I could have my own sheep, comes to the forefront of my mind... perhaps with goats and ducks as well.

I pick up the dream and set it aside deciding that next time around when I come into this world I might line up in the queue that gives me long long legs that finish at my armpits (another life-long dream) and then I might just be able to get over the hurdles… an absolute necessity on a farm - opening hurdles to make an impromptu gate doesn't fit the image when I want to pretend this is where I belong and am truly a part of the scene. I want to be able to swing my ever-so long legs nonchalantly over the five barred gate with ease… though maybe not with my arthritic knees methinks.

Off-Piste Trial

I have got more confidence with all I've learned at the clinics and I've begun to attempt a few more trials. Most times my confidence is misplaced and we certainly don't shine. They're not big well known trials but smaller novice level ones. I find it difficult to try to be confident; to stride out hoping that maybe this time we'll work more as a partnership and come off the field feeling we're progressing.

Harriet has always shown me clearly that, for her, gathering hundreds of sheep in a big field is what it's all about, this trials game with just five sheep over there is a somewhat futile exercise, why bother with so few?

However, today she seems more excited on the trial field than usual... really keen to get going. Despite the onlookers leaning on the fence, my spirits lift as I walk to the judge's van telling myself to be positive and believe we really can do this; perhaps at last she's learning what trialling is all about. As she goes off to our left on my come-bye command, she's really doing a great outrun, wider than usual without me having to push her out... I'm thinking to myself "she's going well, she's really going to do it, we really are beginning to get this"... my heart rate picks up pace along with her stride.

As I'm expecting her to continue round on the comebye to get behind the five waiting sheep, yes she really is going to get that pear shape everyone keeps talking about - yes yes... but oh no, I suddenly realise it isn't going to happen. Harriet continues straight on and bustles through the hedge, at the end of the field, streaking across an empty field behind the course. (Who said she has no gears and Beardies don't speed up like Border Collies do?)

Having left the post, I turn to raise my hand to the judge. This is a rather redundant indicator to the judge that I have retired from the trial since my dog has completely disappeared from the field, but it is trialling etiquette so I'd better try and obey at least one of the rules. Blowing my stop whistle with as much force as I can muster, I set off for the gap in the hedge to see Harriet disappearing through the hedge over on the far side of the barren field. I raise my eye line, looking up the hill towards the sky-blue horizon; the penny drops, she's heading for a very large number of sheep scattered over the steep hillside beyond. I'm puffing my way across in her wake... she completes a brilliant gather, (shame the judge won't see that...) I'm verging on panic questioning whose sheep these are that Harriet is fetching down the hill straight to me; well off at the back, flanking left and right keeping them all together, all moving steadily, all happening with ease. I begin to get my breath back as I call her round on the aaway. She takes my flank and I keep her coming all the way round, stopping her in front of me facing forward onto 'her' sheep and, on my command, she walks on driving the whole flock back up the hill.

I call her off with a "that'll do" and she returns straight to my side. As we walk together back over the empty field, Harriet behaves for all the world as though she's won first prize; jigging about at my side, her upturned face doing her very best to get me to join in the jollity. She is clearly totally unaware of my dejection with me wondering quite where I went wrong this time.

As I come back through the hedge at the top of the trial field I see the judge raise his loudhailer and his voice rings out. A ripple of mocking applause echoes from the spectator fence as his words resound "disqualified for leaving the course!" I can't resist laughing, after all we've been gone twenty minutes!

Back to the drawing board then. As I disappear to the car I reflect on just how difficult it is to improve in this sport. Yes we are learning and improving gradually but so slowly that I begin to sympathise with Eddie the Eagle and his lack of snow covered mountains from which to practise his ski jumps.

There are definitely times when I felt that not only are we failing to advance in any direction but that we may actually be regressing in ability... not even treading water and standing still although there are many times when experience in treading *in* water and developing a more than close relationship with its ever present partner - mud, is definitely something we have achieved.

I have discovered this is not a skill for the fainthearted. I'm beginning to realise my urgent need for more access to sheep to be able to learn for myself what the real work of the shepherd is.

I'm labouring at this the wrong way round, trialling with a dog is ultimately a way of 'showing off' the dog and the shepherd's abilities together... refining and transferring his everyday sheep farming skills to the sports arena, to the sheepdog trial. I'm trying to run before I can walk, or rather, to trial before we can shepherd!

Pastures New

Sometimes when you're really stuck, when hope diminishes; when the doldrums strike and no progress seems to be happening in any direction, something unexpected happens.

I had known for some time what a mountain we were trying to climb and at the same time was realising that Harriet was at her best, and at her happiest, when she was working large flocks of sheep as we had access to sometimes on the farm where the clinics were held. Occasionally, our trainer at the clinic would leave others of the group practising some trial technique and would take me off to another part of the farm to see and try the sort of work he knew to be more suited to a Beardie's skills. Here I was able to appreciate more her natural instincts and I grew to share her love for that bigger, less exacting talent.

Alongside this acknowledgement, it reinforced for me just how uncompetitive I am. I really didn't have this drive to win at any trial. I wanted to get better, I wanted us to improve our ability to work in partnership, to manage some stage of the trial course we'd previously been unable to complete; but for me it wasn't ever about winning or even being placed... it was much more about mastering the sheepherding art.

To find myself involved in a hobby where three live beings were involved, me, Harriet and sheep was fascinating, all absorbing and fun, but to compete with those three elements and turn it into a competitive sport didn't really float my boat (or shear my sheep) I'd always been much more interested in watching and clapping the winner of any sport than wanting to be in that position myself. I always wanted the person to whom the prize would mean so much to win it because they wanted it so much.

The challenge for me was always against myself... I got real satisfaction if, as a partnership, we got better, even in our practise sessions somehow the winning or losing cluttered up the event for me. Maybe I'd developed the trait from my schooldays where I remember being a failure at most things so perhaps I learned never to aim too high. Whatever it was it has served me well. I was always more comfortable in my work life to be working at a level I knew I could do well rather than always striving and pushing myself to perform beyond my level of competence... and that made me happy. I can't remember who it was who said "Life is full of challenges, being happy shouldn't be one of them" – I believe that.

Then from nowhere something unexpected happened, something wonderful and full of promise. The training clinics that I so looked forward to were inhabited by an eclectic bunch of us sheepdog addicts. A real mixture of backgrounds and ages, many of us travelling considerable distances to the farm that offered us fields and sheep to learn on, gathering at an early hour ready to avidly begin talking dogs and sheepherding again... our shared passion. These training clinics are held at a busy working sheep farm way out in the countryside with a generous farmer who is interested in keeping the trialling sport alive.

Annie, who I'd met here a few times and who had two really good Border Collies asked if I would like to visit her on her farm which she said was only forty minutes away from where I live. "I've got sheep" she said "Bring Harriet and give her some practise". Delighted and excited as I was, I had no idea just what a difference this invitation was to make to my life and I've never been really able to find words to sufficiently describe what a gift this has been. In so many ways it has brought such joy into the whole experience for me... not the least of which has been a really cherished friendship. There's something very special about a friend who cares enough about you and your dog that they allow you both access to their sheep. I was once told that old friends are the best unless you're able to find a new one that's fit to make an old one out of! How great is that, a friend who wants to talk sheep and dogs as much as I do.

Annie and her partner Dan run a mixed farm with cows, arable and 1500 sheep. The sheep are grazed over many huge and varied fields with wooded areas, large bridle ways, streams and lakes... an extent of countryside terrain that I've never before had the privilege of frequenting other than to cross its public footpaths.

The experiences Harriet and I have been able to explore here over the months have been immeasurable and make me give thanks time and again for this windfall of good luck I've been offered by Annie.

Now I'm here, I recognise even more acutely how difficult this art of sheep herding is without frequent access to sheep... and inexperienced beginners like me also need the constant guiding hand showing me almost at every turn where I'm wrong and how to get it right. More than that, the progress is so slow that sometimes it's unrecognisable and I need to be reminded of where we were both were and how far we've come. This encouragement becomes my anchor and each time I return home again I make notes to hold onto on rubbish days when neither myself or Harriet seem to get anything right, when I feel this really is a task beyond my ability, a learning curve beyond my capabilities. These are days when I feel that Harriet has not been given a fair chance, when I know that with a more capable owner she would have become a useful sheep dog, but with me as her shepherd she is destined to never reach her potential. But with all of those experiences, I now have the opportunity to take what I learned at the sheepdog training clinics and work at putting it into practice.

I'm not sure who struggled most when we were first at Annie's. She was always so encouraging when I seemed to end up with Harriet always losing the sheep and one of Annie's brilliant dogs collecting them all together again for us to have another go. I was in awe watching each of Annie's dogs and learning her training techniques. She has to explain all the details to me every time explaining where, why, what and how it's all coming together. I feel I can't grasp it all quickly enough... let alone replicate with Harriet anything I've seen.

Sometimes I've gone home deflated, absolutely sure we're actually going backwards and failing to put anything I've seen or learned into practice. Even then, on our worst days, when I feel it will never come right; when we both climb into the car to drive home soaked to the skin with the wipers on at double speed... even then I can't wait to come back for more.

I'm beginning to wonder about this sheepdog farm life that I'm now trying to part of. I had imagined retired life was straightforward and uncomplicated. Just as I had expected in a previous life to walk hand in hand into old age with my marriage partner and that certainly didn't happen!

I had somehow visualised when I left my district nursing career that with the lack of the necessary structure required when at work, I would go forward with my new 'significant other, Harriet, into an easy dog-walking calling and we would wander the footpaths of the surrounding countryside in a relaxed, unstructured way, my mind perhaps working just hard enough to contemplate what I might like for supper.

Instead I find myself trying to learn a craft for which I've had no previous knowledge let alone training and, what's more, with Harriet, who seems to have more of a natural leaning towards what's happening than I do.

It's all somewhat different from my previous vocation... where yes I worked just as hard but I seemed to have much more instinct for the profession I was following; where to visit a patient in his hour of need in his own home, to convince him to accept and agree to a necessary treatment was infinitely easier than 'visiting' a herd of sheep in their 'home', the field, persuading them into a pen and convincing every one of them to accept treatment of diseases such as fly-strike or worms (when they are all needle phobic)... "Please will you go nicely down this run now, and through the footbath, no honestly it really won't hurt, it might just sting a bit."

I was glad to find that nail clipping was considered less necessary with large outside flocks ... foot bathing being more common... or do these tasks go in and out of favour in the farming world? Tasks certainly do in health care; everyone has their tonsils out at age two and then no-one is allowed them out 'till they're ten! Getting to grips with nail clipping needs a bit more strength than I'd needed in a former life... however old or knackered were the feet and toes I'd been privy to, I never had to roll any patient on to their back and grip them between my knees to inspect them!

I am beginning to spot the sheep who are limping as we send them down the run but haven't as yet developed the seemingly fluid movement that Annie achieves flicking the sheep on to its haunches where poorly feet are now within reach for her to deal with despite flailing legs in all directions; it's quite an art. Foot scald and foot rot are common foot infections to be aware of it seems which isn't surprising when you see the cleft in the divided hoof which provides the perfect place for mud to get trapped and so allow any bacteria to flourish. I understand that running them through the foot bath is what keeps these infections under control and it really does seem to be effective with the limping sheep seeming much more comfortable afterwards.

Sometimes if there was any sort of cut on the foot, perhaps from a flint, a blue antibiotic spray can be applied to assist healing.

* * *

As he limps off with a bright blue foot I have to remind myself that he's OK and really doesn't need a sterile dressing pad and 3 inch bandage from toe to knee, (applied of course from inside to outside of the leg with graduated pressure to avoid undue swelling) and a request to please keep the area dry until I return for further inspection... old habits die hard.

* * *

Actually I'm amazed at how relatively unaffected any sheep seems to be by an infected limb and how little attention it requires; any wound seems to be quick to heal despite the muddiest conditions... *maybe I missed a trick and should have carried a bright blue penicillin spray in my district nursing bag!*

I heard a discussion on one farm where we went trialling about 'pharmacy farming' where the debate seemed to be about the pros and cons of more and more drugs being used in sheep and cattle rearing. As an untrained observer of farm life, I've been surprised at how seldom and how few antibiotics and medicaments seem to be necessary in caring for sheep and how well they cope with the outdoor elements of cold, wet and mud, indeed all weathers.

As I spend more time on the farm with Annie, I find myself more engaged with the whole farming scene than I expected... a sentiment that seems to be mimicked by Harriet who seems increasingly to enter into days here with more determination and enthusiasm than ever she did at the prospect of trialling. Learning a job of work seems to be what interests her, rather than being expected to display talent (or otherwise!) on a trial field.

She shows me this so clearly sometimes when I really feel we're learning together, when I'm getting a bit more of this 'sheep sense' they talk about and Harriet really seems to see the point of the job I'm asking her to do….all of this with Annie guiding both of us on how to do it. I do wonder sometimes if Annie suspects the sheep are easier to manage than me when she'll be moving me yet again into the right position to allow the sheep to be where we need them.

Today we needed to take a smallish flock of about forty sheep from one field to another by way of a gap in the fencing. Annie knew this would be tricky because she let me know that these sheep had never gone this way before, previously frequently being herded to the other end of the big sixty acre field, downhill to a bridle way. So she positioned me by the gap and I sent Harriet to gather the sheep and steadily bring them to me. They were quite feisty and I needed to hold her off at the back of the sheep once they were gathered while we waited for the first few to begin to go through the fence. Harriet then did throw me a glance as if to say "Are you sure you know what you're doing, holding these sheep here?" But she gently nudged them using those lovely square flanks we'd been learning and practising, just encouraging them through; good job Harriet. I give her a 'well done' pat and stroke.

Square flanks involve the dog turning directly off the sheep, on command, out to the left or right, sometimes just the turn of the dogs head will be sufficient to nudge the first sheep to turn the way you want; a move both Harriet and I continue to grapple with.

We are learning, Lady H (Annie's pet name for Harriet!)… Lady H and I, to begin to manage just a few of these farm tasks and I catch my breath when we get it right and complete a task.

The Perfect Day

Fantastic day today on the farm, two big hills dipping down into a valley, a bright winter's morning, crisp frost still holding on over the grass that edges the surrounding woodland. Annie, myself and Harriet walk up almost to the top of the steep hills on one side where we can look across to the ascending incline opposite, the other side of the gully. I catch my breath, not only because of the climb, but in part as I turn and take in the magnificent scene; bright blue sky meeting the burnished gold bronze colours of the autumnal trees spilling into the verdant green pasture beneath where three hundred white sheep are quietly grazing. It's one of those moments to capture for the memory bank, the stunning landscape feeding my soul. There is something so quintessentially English about this backdrop, somehow reminiscent of a time when the pace of life was slower.

No, I don't want to go backwards but just occasionally to savour a glimmer of light from the past, showing us a kinder, slower way to live has indeed to be applauded… like right now, simply breathing in this beautiful landscape.

I'm pulled suddenly back to why we are here when Annie asks me to send Harriet to gather the sheep away on the opposite hill. I hesitate, firstly it feels something of an intrusion into this idyllic scene and secondly because of my uncertainty about Harriet's ability (or very probable incompetence) to undertake such a task …the peaceful panorama may shortly be no more.

I summon up my courage as I send her off to my right with an aaway and as much confidence as I'm able to muster, trying really hard to believe in her. Sometimes little miracles happen. It really is at least a reasonable outrun, down my hill into the ravine and up the hill the other side. I realise how steep it is as I watch her flank round the back of the sheep tucking in the sheep at the far end as they begin to gather themselves together on the steep side of the hill. Harriet begins to flank back and forth behind this large group, tucking them in either end of the increasing group at each turn. Sheep resist going downhill, they much prefer to move upwards on any incline. As a result of the pressure exerted by the dog, the sheep form a mass and begin to 'mill' round and round in a circle, each sheep trying to get nearer and nearer the centre of the crowd and 'safety'. Harriet continues to flank left and right continually and I'm beginning to wonder whether they will ever begin to move down to the gully.

It's like watching a slow motion recording as slowly the swirling mass begins to turn their heads down the hill and with Harriet continuing to flank making sure she keeps them all together, they begin to stream down the hill, flowing like a river in increasing numbers along the gully, the river bed.

I'm in awe of what's happening and my feet are glued to my side of the hill until Annie tells me to go down to my left heading for the gate and pen where we want all three hundred sheep to be corralled before encouraging them all through the footbath.

Once again I didn't manage to get myself quite into the right position to assist her, but for once my mistakes don't matter at all even to me because I'm so excited and inordinately proud of my very own dog looking for all the world like a proper farm dog! Harriet continues her job, despite the fact that I'm in the wrong place (How the hell does Annie have any patience left when she tries so hard continually to get me to 'feel' where I should be to both help Harriet and not block the sheep and I just don't seem to learn)

However, nothing will spoil this moment as I close the gate and bend down to ruffle Harriet's coat, with her tail wagging and her bright eyes just saying "See I can really do it when you give me the work I'm made for".

We walk together to the horse trough where I break the fragile ice for Harriet to slake her thirst. Annie tells me that her two beautiful multitalented border collies would have struggled to accomplish the task that Harriet has just undertaken and while Harriet rolls on her back in a clumpy patch of frosty grass my cheeks flush with pride. At this very moment (and probably *only ever* for this very moment) I am a shepherd and Harriet is a sheepdog... 'my cup runneth over' with joy!

I will never forget this day ...it will always remain a highlight for me. I drive home with Harriet 'out for the count' on the back seat. I feel a glow of unrivalled happiness stirred in with a huge ladle of gratitude that I have been offered this chance... to be able to experience something in retirement that I never saw coming, that I never even knew I wanted, is indeed an intense pleasure given to me first by Harriet... I so love that dog... and then by the fabulous Annie whose place in heaven is surely guaranteed right next to the Arc Angel Gabriel by way of her kindness, perseverance and tolerance... what did I ever do in my past life to deserve such goodness coming my way?

I began to sing out loud to the radio as I drive home. This has been my perfect day; only an interruption over the airwaves announcing the results of a recent study revealing that shortbread is now considered a 'health' food that contains no calories... only this proclamation could have added anything at all to my day... unadulterated gladness right here in this moment.

Until Morning is Nigh

While I was struggling to find a way into working Harriet on sheep I was lucky enough one Spring to be invited down to Wales onto a small sheep farm with about forty ewes. It was lambing time and a great opportunity to be around and, in a small way, to be part of it.

Night duties are clearly destined to follow me into my retirement pastime. There is an eeriness entering a barn in the middle of the night setting my alarm and going out to the barn to see what was happening and stealthily standing motionless in a secluded corner observing the pregnant ewes, watching, waiting, straining to observe each and every one of my charges for signs of labour; considering every movement each one makes, circling, restlessness, seeming unable to settle, scratching at the straw... straining her head backwards, a water bag descending. There was much to learn here in the hush of a cold night, the puffing of hot breath from flared nostrils, the odd bellowing bleat echoing around the barn either announcing a truly established labour or even maybe an untroubled arrival.

My few night visits were uneventful; expectation in the crisp air yes, but gentle and quiet shifts. As I counted my charges, relieved to find yes all thirty were present not all sleeping, but settled with no deliveries looking imminent, so I could make it back to bed before needing to call for a more experienced eye to assess progress and any possible impending delivery. As I tucked myself back under the duvet I remember wondering whether all farmers do night shifts throughout lambing time. I did hear of one barn where they had a pulldown bed for use at lambing time - what luxury.

I doubt if there would have been a plug for my electric over-blanket though...

* * *

It really does remind me of other nights in my nurse training, when I was as inexperienced and mindful of those under my care. Long Nightingale Wards similar in size to this barn with patients in bed either side the complete length of the ward and me left to mind them while my senior went for her break at midnight. All twenty six patients reliant on me as I walked up and down the length of the ward with my torch; alert to every sound and attentive to every restless movement. They were long twelve hour nights where utter fatigue meant giving in and closing your eyelids for a blissful ten seconds wherever you thought you wouldn't be noticed, perhaps walking along a corridor. Memories of the absolute bliss of snatching ten minutes illicit sleep on a hospital trolley on a quiet night when a kindly staff nurse took pity on me as exhaustion overtook my attempts to stay awake

* * *

Here at Annie's, lambing would be happening outdoors, so I was going to be able to compare both indoor and outdoor labouring and lambing. For several weeks we'd been travelling round in the Land Rover over and round large fields with Annie inspecting all the pregnant ewes. We'd sometimes stop in the middle of a field and she would point out a ewe who she'd tell me was in the early stages of labour, showing me what to look for, what were the signs. Once again I'm reminded of how having contact with sheep, being aware of and watching normal sheep behaviour is paramount to begin to recognise the different conduct being displayed that may indicate the onset of labour

There was something very natural about the birthing process out here, watching the ewe wander off to find somewhere on her own, away from the rest of the flock in the field. The meadows were vast, lots of space to get away from the crowd and find your labouring spot and make it your own; choose where you want to be, in a copse of trees, nestled near to the hedge, out in the open, among the bushes or out of sight down in a dip. Sometimes it was really evident that the ewe didn't want an audience and if we were too near and she moved away, she would return to her safe spot when we drove slowly away. She seemed much more likely to get on with the job if she was allowed to stay where she wanted and I noticed that Annie was reluctant to move any ewe who was showing signs of labour unless her chosen patch to give birth was perhaps unsafe and may indeed be even more so after the birth. We did encourage a ewe and her new born twins away from the edge of a river, Annie explaining that the lambs could easily drown if they tumbled into even the shallowest edge of the stream. I felt sorry for the ewe; it looked an ideal delivery suite among the reeds and rushes but she did follow us as we carried the babes by their arms close to the ground while she continued to lick and bleat with her offspring and settled in a scrub area not too far away.

We moved on watching for more ewes, identifying those who were restless, often pawing the ground, getting up and down or maybe exhibiting more advanced signs of progress, lying down, her legs to the side throwing her head back staring at the stars and curling her top lip as she strains, maybe displaying that most obvious indication, the water bag hanging down.

Comparing birthing in the barn and out in the field it felt as though the sheep got on with the job of labouring more readily away from prying eyes on the hills but with some of the inclement weather days I couldn't help feeling for the little newborne lambs as the rain poured down and the wind didn't seem to let up. I did notice how quickly out in the field the mum seemed to lick her lamb dry, protecting him from the elements.

This 'in the field' lambing appeared somehow a more natural experience to my untrained eye... not so sterile, not so monitored... there was limited cleaning of pens with lime ready for the next labouring ewe and less immediate cleansing of the umbilicus than happened in the barn. But then out in the open perhaps less need for such meticulous cleansing? But then I know nothing about how these two different ways of lambing translates into survival or infection rates.

* * *

I find myself sometimes comparing indoor lambing to the hospital delivery system whereas out in the field was the 'home' or 'community 'delivery. The pens in the barn could be compared to the beds in a labouring or post- natal ward.

* * *

Out in the field there was certainly less interference in the process as I witnessed it. However, my indoor lambing experience was not only decidedly limited but also involved small numbers of ewes. Perhaps in large lambing barns there was also less interference... and maybe there is a considerable difference in 'casualty' rates between barn and outdoor lambing or indeed between small and large flock birthing.

My own responses quite liked the routine of cleaning in the barn, of moving ewe and lamb from a single pen into a nursery pen with several others before, in another few days, going out into a small field area during the day and being brought back into the barn at night

* * *

I certainly felt that home deliveries were not quite as sanitised as the conveyor belt structure of the hospital birth .... Indeed, probably there was less chance of picking up infections at home, away from the crowded ward.

* * *

It was quite a different experience with 'out in the field' lambing where I was learning to look for different things. When I came to see lambing on a larger scale and outside with Annie, I saw night time lambing differently. Early morning counting was more about how many lambs belonged to each ewe. Sometimes it was very clear who belonged to whom... brilliant mums with two or sometimes three beautiful lambs all trotting along happily, well fed and bonded. More often in a triplet delivery one lamb would be frail and a bit poorly looking. Annie explained that with each ewe only having two teats it was common for a third lamb to need help and she would scoop the unfortunate lamb up and put him in my lap in front in the Land Rover.

Sometimes he may be fostered on by a mum whose own lamb had failed to thrive, or more likely be part of the nursery group in the shed in the yard to be bottle fed... a job I undertook with pleasure. I heard stories of lambs being saved from sure death by warming them up in the plate warming oven of the old range; but things had moved on and we now had lamps that hovered over the poorly lambs, warming up many a wet cold lamb we rescued on an early morning round. He'd then be nursed back to health and strength and be loudly demanding a feed as I entered the nursery barn at lunch time.

Great learning times for me watching Annie with her knowledge and intuition attending to a newly delivered ewe and her lambs. She expertly used one of her dogs to hold the ewe while making sure the teats were clear and the rich colostrum was flowing well. We watched as lambs locked on and, with jiggling tails, filled their tummies. It looks very similar to encouraging a new born human infant to latch on to a full breast before mother's milk has 'let down'… but I didn't ever need a Harriet to control a human mother, who was usually more than ready to accept my help.

* * *

I couldn't resist noting how much similarity there is between the labouring habits of both ewes and women… and indeed the comparison between barn and field delivery units juxtaposed against the hospital or home delivery keeps bobbing about in my head as I watch and, in a decidedly limited way, help with lambing.

* * *

I'm less confident that'll I'll be able to transfer my midwifery skills to aid a labouring ewe with a difficult delivery. I'm anxious to try but don't yet know how to manage two advancing cloven hooves - but I'm learning.

* * *

I have, on the district in times gone by, managed the odd breech delivery rather than only the more usual head first birth.

And there was the odd 'footling breech' presentation that required pushing a foot back while encouraging the breech to descend into the birth canal... maybe in time I'll learn what to do with hooves!

* * *

I must say the joy when watching the new lamb at minutes old struggle to its feet and suckle is almost as exhilarating as helping a human babe take its first breath.

I had always thought lambing only happened in the Spring, and indeed on many farms this is the case but on Annie and Dan's farm there is almost all year round lambing. While still the majority of the ewes are tupped in early November some are put to the ram earlier giving rise to a limited amount of lambs being born in the early months of the year. When these first lambs are braving the cold and rain, I'm always amazed to see how well they cope. As we enter the frosty starched field early on a January morning we sometimes see one of the early lambing ewes giving her undivided attention to the lamb keeping him from becoming chilly. The warm rounded tummy full of colostrum indicating his chances of survival are good. It seems that whenever the lamb is born if he doesn't get sufficient of this creamy new milk in the first twenty four hours he is almost destined to struggle to survive and will most probably fail and die. While watching a lamb get to his feet for the first time in the snow is magically special. The greater part of lambing continues to happen at the more conventional time, a couple or so months later heralding both Spring and the warmer weather.

Something to Bleat About

I heard recently that learning a foreign language when you're advancing in years is one of the best ways to maintain the brain pathways and so avoid the onset of dementia I'm beginning to wonder whether the new terminology I'm struggling to understand and grasp in my new world will in any way serve the same purpose.

Come-bye and aaway I managed; clockwise, C for left and clockwise, A for right and anticlockwise. Mind you, when I did finally managed to reach the dizzy heights of the smallest of sheepdog trials, I would never have believed it could be so difficult to remember right from left when you're out there on the course... with the tension of a trial run exacerbating the number of times I've known precisely where I want to send Harriet but exactly the opposite command falls out of my mouth!

Also the clockwise C and the anticlockwise A aren't quite so easy to remember when you are directing your dog coming towards you. This is because Harriet's come-bye, in other words her left, when she's coming towards me is on my right when she's facing me.

I'm driving home from a particularly joyful day where Harriet and I have been taking part in a very small way with lambing outside on a lovely sunny day in the beautiful Buckinghamshire countryside. I find myself juggling with the jargon I've heard, trying to put meaning to what I think are words used indicating the age of sheep.

There are lambs of course who I think become shearlings between their first and second shearing who then become gimmers (who are female lambs that are to be kept as breeding ewes) and then hoggets (who may be male or female destined for slaughter). There's something about store lambs too, I'm not quite sure where they fit into the scheme of things but I know they are lambs that get fattened up ready for culling.

I remember having a quiet giggle one day when Annie was having real difficulty getting a ewe to accept her lamb and let it feed. In fact the ewe was so stroppy she was trying to butt Annie as well as the lamb when, while she was down on her knees, eye to eye with the ewe, in a frustrated voice, I heard her saying to the ewe "You'd better behave or I'll send you down to the cull field" Well she must have understood, she finally decided she would let the lamb feed after all.

Then with the passing of time both ewes and rams become 'broken- mouthed', sheep who begin to lose their teeth, usually about 6 years of age. I have particular sympathy with this group ….. my teeth have been very troublesome probably from the time I was about 6yrs old; but at least I started with top and bottom teeth … sheep only ever have a lower case.

These old ladies are usually brought down from their heft (an area of land, traditionally in the uplands, where sheep remain in a space that has no physical boundaries but they do not stray beyond it) I think there might be a cross over here with these senior sheep citizens, where they become draft ewes that are not going to be put to the tup (the ram) any more so won't have any more lambs and will be sold to farmers on lower ground where the terrain and weather are less challenging. Again we have things in common …. they may not have a bus pass like me but I shall no longer produce off-spring and my knees are certainly finding hills more demanding. However, I think this group may then be fattened up prior to being sold as mutton… fattening up is a likely possibility in my case (in fact I'm failing miserably to halt its progress) but selling me for mutton is perhaps unlikely...

I think I might prefer being 'put out to grass' when I'm old and cranky rather than being moved into a care home... as long as it's not the cull field. Even with no teeth and aching knees, as a sheep, I would at least have the freedom to push off to a comfy corner of the field, lie under a hedge and maybe swap stories with some friendly old ewe; both of us determinedly steering clear of some miserable, interfering bad tempered old codger of a ram. In a care home I wouldn't be able to escape, being positioned daily in the same chair in the same circle in the same dining room being bored rigid and having to pretend I'm grateful for the opportunity... and I'd be expected to go there without my dog.

I might become 'cast' in protest were I subjected to that indignity; a cast ewe is a term used for a sheep lying over on its back unable to get to its feet

Anyway I think I'm fairly 'hefted' now... I don't need physical barriers to keep me here. I've always wondered if I had a gene missing because I never really had a zest for travel even though everyone seems to think that 'seeing the world' is what retirement is made for. Who wants to travel or to stay anywhere without their beloved pet?

And it's not just with sheep where I've found a new language to learn, sheepdog birthing seems to have a lingo of its own. I have to say I still struggle when listening while at trials... "that's a good pup you know, lots of possible potential, sired by so and so's Greg dog who was *out of* so and so's bitch, did very well in the national that bitch did". It's never 'born to' or 'a son of'... somehow '*out of*' doesn't sound quite right. If we labelled a new borne baby with the tag round its ankle saying 'out of Peggy Smith', it would add an impropriety to the proceedings I feel.

But then I can't imagine any prospective human mum being described as 'bagging up' as her breast milk begins to 'let down' but it's a phrase that very aptly describes those birthing processes in the ewe. Even more unfamiliar to my ears was the expression I overheard recently referring to a mare in foal where the owner was talking about who she'd been 'covered by'…, perhaps an even more unseemly term were it ever to be used on the birth certificate!

I do come more into my own whenever we need to tend to a poorly sheep with sticky eyes or other signs of infection. I have found I'm still fairly dexterous at drawing-up the necessary antibiotic into the syringe and can deliver an injection to a sheep without too much difficulty… all under the watchful eye of Annie who of course both catches and holds the ewe ready for her dose. When Annie herself medicates several sheep I can load syringes with the correct amount of whatever she requires which enables things to keep moving on a busy morning. It feels good to be useful and perhaps make-up for the time wasted when either Harriet or I, lose the sheep we're gathering or taking an interminable amount of time to do a job which would have taken Annie and any one of her dogs five minutes, even with her most inexperienced recruit.

I was fascinated to see how rapid the response can be to an injection of calcium in the hypo calcaemic ewe. In late pregnancy or early lactation, sometimes a ewe would exhibit extreme listlessness that very quickly reversed when the subcutaneous injection of calcium was given. From lethargy and fatigue that, if untreated, would continue to unconsciousness, she would struggle to her feet while we watched, looking around for her lamb and ambling off with her charge in a few minutes, in no time at all… indeed in two shakes of a lambs tail. I had witnessed a very similar response, on occasion, in patients when disease had caused a depletion of calcium in the blood. Rapidly, a previously exhausted, apparently depressed patient would begin to feel better within a short amount of time and while not exactly scampering away like the sheep, there was often evidence of improvement within minutes sometimes.

* * *

It's seems I inevitably relate any medical knowledge my aging brain has managed to hold on to and I find myself comparing it to similar symptoms displayed in ailing animals and observing the treatment cycle. Unfortunately, this leads me to wanting return to a field at the end of the morning, just to check on a poorly sheep... a bit like making a detour at the end of a day's district nursing to enable me, on my way home, just to check that the pain relief I'd administered earlier to a patient, had indeed taken effect as I intended.

* * *

I suppose the nutrients in the local chalky soil keeps the calcium levels in most sheep hunky dory at least most of the time. I'd like to think the chalk mounds that I fall over with undignified regularity do serve a useful purpose. Either chalk or turnips combine with my arthritic knees to catch me out on quite a few occasions particularly since learning to shepherd does involve a considerable amount of walking backwards, with the dog behind the flock of sheep bringing them to you... in Harriet's and my case, more rapidly than I might have chosen if I'd managed to blow my whistle command sooner and Lady H had not chosen to play deaf! To be fair, Harriet usually manages to avoid trampling me with the sheep when I've fallen!

* * *

I will only ever admit to 'falling over' I refuse ever to say or have anyone else use the term 'had a fall'. There is a difference; the latter is used in the medical field almost as a diagnosis in itself, meaning "this is the beginning of the end now, this is where deterioration begins..."she's <u>had a fall</u>!" Well in this 'field' I might fall over but never let it be said 'I've had a fall'.

I guess I'm sensitive to the comment only because I knew it so often to be true in elderly patients I'd nursed who, following broken hips and such like, never quite made it back to full mobility again. Being unable to ignore such facts means that, despite my creaking knees, I'll only ever admit to 'falling over', I'll never 'have a fall'... a subtle difference in the use of words but a big difference in meaning between the two statements.

* * *

I think I may finally have learned the difference between hay and silage, they are both cut grass but the silage is wrapped and fermented, keeping all the goodness and nutrients, to feed the sheep through the winter. Straw is the dry stalks from cereal plants and is used as bedding for animals when they're in the barn.

I'm openly declaring now and for all time that none of the facts here can be depended upon for accuracy or even truth; it's simply how I've heard, misheard or interpreted this new language going on around me in this foreign land or rather farmyard! However, I'm really just enjoying leaving all that medical jargon and annoying abbreviations behind as I pick up new colourful verbiage... and hopefully delaying the creeping forgetfulness that threatens to merge with the confusion.

Counting Sheep

Personally insomnia has never been a problem for me and as my head descends towards the pillow, so my eyelids close. I do however have a friend whose experiences in the sleep department are exactly opposite to mine and she describes getting into bed and laying her head on the pillow as being equivalent to a light switch going on. She further assures me that counting sleep is a totally useless strategy to employ when desperate tiredness and wakefulness go hand in hand... so much for old wives tales - I did suggest envisioning jiggling lambs' tales but that didn't go down very well!

* * *

Such a relatively short time ago if I'd been asked what sort of sheep I liked or would choose to own, the question itself would have stumped me. All sheep were much the same I thought, fluffy with a leg at either corner, mostly white with the occasional black lamb amongst the pack. I now find myself able to identify a few makes and models and speculating on which variety I might choose should I ever find myself with my own small holding. It's the stuff of mind meanderings in the wee small hours and, for me, works far better than actually trying to count a large number of sheep as a way of slipping back into nocturnal slumbers on a rare, restless night. It's certainly an improvement on disturbed nights in my past life where it was patients I would be counting and adding to my ever increasing fictitious list of visits which just *had* to be made by morning.

* * *

Night nursing of any sort, hospital or district, has a special feel and quality about it that while it's difficult to define, many nurses will admit to. Often barriers are down, with fears heightened for patients in the darkest hours. Some of the deepest, most sincere 'healing moments' between nurse and patient can happen on a night shift where maybe simply a steadfast, caring presence allows a patient to utter words that have been unthinkable in daylight hours. Now alone, stripped bare of pretence it may be possible to stand alongside a helpless patient, to validate previously unspoken feelings and with touch, caring words or simply by 'being there', something happens; maybe strength to face tomorrow or courage to go forward.... but it happens. To be part of that exchange, perhaps by simply discerning the relief experienced by a concerned relative as you arrive to make a late night call, is indeed a privilege that few are offered by way of the job they do.

* * *

My imaginary farm exists often in my head. I'm not sure whether it's that I really believe one day I'll return in another guise to have another go at life or whether I just mull over what it would have been like to have had a different work life, maybe with a field of Herdwicks, definitely my favourite breed. They are born black with white ear tips but change colour as they age becoming greyish with a white frosted looking head. Beardies change colour too, their black coat changes to grey, although, in

Harriet's case, some parts of her remain more black than most others of her breed.

Herdwicks exude character somehow with teddy bear fluffy legs and knocked knees. They are a hardy mountain breed known for their ability to cope with inclement weather conditions and with a propensity to survive with minimal supplementary feeding when needs must. They tend to birth with little interference and a day old lamb with a good mother is said to be almost imperishable whatever the weather.

Mind you, after my one and only attempt at shearing I do have a soft spot for Soays as a breed of sheep because they do the sensible thing and shed their fleeces with absolutely no help from mankind... although I have to say 'shabby chic' doesn't work as a description of their dress code... 'over the top shabby' is definitely more accurate. Their coats shed in a very tatty, disorganised way and long strings of partially shed straggly broken fleeces seem to be the end result; not a particularly attractive dress code.

I visited a farm in Lancashire where I was lucky enough to be given a small group of sheep to work. What a perfect holiday; staying in a lovely converted barn with some sheep to call my own for a whole week. It was a farm with dry stone walls round many of its fields. One morning I took Harriet into our field and I sent her to pick up the small flock of sheep all laying in the far corner. As Harriet approached and they all got to their feet, still curled up on the ground in the middle of them was a week old lamb. Within a few minutes the farmer was coming round on his quadbike looking for the escapee. He said that there was a ewe bleating loudly a couple of fields away earnestly looking for her lamb so he was travelling his fields counting sheep and lambs trying to find this one. He told me that the lambs were always clambering up on these walls and, because many of them were quite wide across the top, they often trotted off and got themselves lost. I just liked the way this little group had snuggled round protecting him from harm overnight until he was returned 'home' the following morning.

So sometimes it's not so much counting sheep as pairing up the right lamb or lambs with the right ewe. If they've been born in the barn they usually all have a number sprayed on their coat to assist with the task. But if they're born outside more independently they seem to sort themselves out in the end. There have been several times when we've driven into large fields with very scattered flocks where an adventurous lamb appears to have got himself lost and we've stayed in the Land Rover watching the pantomime play out. Usually this loudly bleating lamb runs about all over the field trying to join a ewe and maybe her singleton only to be turned away with 'a flea in his ear' by the ewe. As he becomes more frantic Annie will sit patiently, exhorting me to wait and watch while she turns the engine off and scans the area. She'll then point out a ewe with probably one maybe two lambs in tow, start murmuring her own noises as she travels several hundred yards across the field to the panicking lamb. It's a sweet sight to watch both see each other, with mum calling her errant offspring back across a little ditch between two trees and her continue with her little family clustered around her.

When the race or run and gate are used to count and separate ewes and lambs at weaning time, the noise is loud and, for me, 'feels' more painful than ringing did... baby forcibly separated from mum. For the first day or two the sound of bleating fills the air; mothers bleating for their lambs and lambs bleating for their mothers. It doesn't last for long and the ewes often seem relieved to be able to rest after the effort of rearing lambs while the lambs begin to fatten up on lush new grass.

The lambs seem more insistent about wanting to stay with their mum than the mum does. The ewe seems to accept the situation sooner than the lamb, enjoying rest and food and gaining energy before tupping comes round again I suspect. The lambs take longer to adapt and often there are attempts by groups or a 'gang' of lambs to escape and search for the field with the ewes in, with attempts being made to break in under the gate to find mum and home.

* * *

I can't help comparing this state of affairs with what many of us human mothers experience now, with many of our offspring being somewhat reluctant to leave home. Well, actually for many of us, they do leave but they keep coming back. I 'laboured' for quite a while under the misapprehension that after our children reached the age of eighteen they left home... not so these days it seems. I discovered having brought up four, I was never quite sure how many I had... they left and returned for quite some time before really leaving the nest.

Of course we love them, and want them to return home often to visit but, listening to friends, separation anxiety raises its head for many at the suggestion of finding their own home and feeding themselves! I'm not sure I hankered to regain bodily condition by the autumn like the ewe and my young developed culinary talents early, probably due to my lack of enthusiasm for slaving over a hot stove (I have friends who like reading recipe books in their spare time, can you believe it?) but in my family, free lodging was obviously appealing.

Lambs when weaned have to say goodbye to not only the nourishment of a constant milk supply from mum, but also the comfort of 'staying at home'. They make a bit of a noise about it all but quickly settle to chomping on the fresh green grass, chewing the cud and curling up with their chums. I haven't noticed any chewing of the cud amongst my own offspring, but take away pizzas to share with mates seemed to be high on the menu when they first left home... weaned on takeaways.

* * *

I used to be largely unaware of sheep until lambing time came around. Fields with sheep in were like a backdrop to rural living... almost scattered over the background canvas of a countryside painting with the subject of the picture featuring prominently in the foreground. Lambing time was when sheep become more noticeable, when fields celebrate gambolling, prancing lambs. My attention was first drawn to sheep by Harriet's wide-eyed undivided attention through fences on our daily walks but even then I'm not sure I gave any thought to what happened to sheep for the rest of the year. Yes, at some time their coats would be sheared but I think I imagined the rest of the year they happily wandered all day munching in grassy fields. When I learned they only had a lower set of teeth and no uppers, I realised a lot of munching time would be needed to stave off hunger for even the smallest stomach.

As well as matching lambs to their mum when they wander I also began to find out that all sheep seem to have a propensity to escape. A penchant for what's in the next field rather than their own seems to drive them on and then often several others try to use the same escape route. Sometimes a walker tramping the local footpaths would contact saying there was a sheep stuck in a hedge or a fence and we'd be off in Annie's trusty transport to investigate and retrieve the truant. Some were really stuck, tied up in brambles making rescue increasingly difficult with the sheep often panicking herself deeper into trouble as we tried to rescue her.

So I learned about capturing ewes who have been seen and noted as escapees, and all about it often being a more intricate task than I would have expected but what about those missing from the flock but who are unaccounted for... just 'missing in action'?

One time, Annie had been working with her dogs in one field while I was working with Harriet in the next door field on a small group of sheep, doing some training for a future small trial. Harriet enjoyed working on large flocks much more where she could pretend she was a full time farm dog (and I could pretend I was a shepherd and I knew what I was doing!) When it came to doing some schooling with her keeping her driving lines straight, staying well off the sheep, making it all look easy, Harriet often looked at me as though she was saying ... " look why do we want to bother with just these, let's go and find a proper flock". Anyway we managed quite a good session with her reluctantly towing the line, turning the small group around me quite nicely after an almost respectable practise outrun and lift. I opened the gate and she steadily took them through at a good pace to join others in the big field.

Quite a good session I thought when I saw Annie gesticulating at me as she raised her voice calling "Where's the other one... you've left one behind; you started with eight!" I ran back with Harriet into the small field and began to search... castigating myself for not even knowing how many sheep I started with and certainly no recollection of losing one. Annie drove up through the gate, stopped and urged me to hop in saying we'd find her together, I was convinced there were no sheep hiding anywhere.

I've been so impressed on so many occasions to note how sensitive Annie's instinct is when dealing with the sheep; whether it's her stopping and staring at a pregnant ewe when there's nothing, absolutely nothing, to see and yet Annie 'feels' she's about to labour or will not mother-up well. Here she was looking closely along a thick wide hedge between two fences and sure enough in the dense, thickest part of the hedge, there was the errant ewe. I knew Harriet hadn't hassled or harried the sheep... I was animatedly explaining to Annie how Harriet couldn't have chased her in there... I'd been watching her too closely. "Oh no it wasn't her I'm sure; that sheep's an awkward old thing she's done it deliberately and got herself well and truly stuck now". Not only could Annie recognise any particular sheep out of the thousand or so they had on the farm, but she'd sensed where she would be when I didn't even recognise I'd lost her and certainly couldn't find her. It occurred to me how hopeless I was at even counting the sheep I was working with. We actually left her there and Annie rescued her much later when she'd made no attempt to come out and I felt guilty for having caused her extra work and dispirited knowing that I had not even realised she'd escaped. Not a good day that one, I felt totally incompetent.

However, each and every day brings its own rewards, be they ups or downs.

Much later on, when I wasn't quite so inept, on one of my farming days came more learning but all wrapped up in sudden unexpected fun... and indeed it truly was enacted out 'farther down the road'! One morning we were in the Land Rover bumbling over a rather sodden field looking at some new baby lambs attempting to steady themselves as they struggled to their feet in the mud, when Annie got a phone call telling her about an escapee ewe from another flock quite a distance from where we were working.

As we headed off on our escapee escapade, Annie set the scene for me telling me where the ewe had been seen outside the main field that held a large flock of sheep. She had been spotted trotting around in and out of a disused barn and vacant yard, trying to find her way to join her mates in the adjoining field.

On arrival she wasn't immediately visible and even when we did catch sight of her she darted off around hidden corners cleverly evading us both while bleating loudly. Suddenly she raced past us jumping frantically as she headed out of the main gate and on to the narrow lane. We were hoping she'd turn and head down the hill which would perhaps encourage her towards other sheep in a lower field. However, this was not to be, displaying the usual sheep reluctance to head downhill, she turns uphill at a 'rate of knots' with us in the Land Rover in hot pursuit. Unfortunately, the narrow lane afforded us absolutely no opportunity to overtake the errant ewe and no evidence at all of even the smallest passing place. Annie tried to steer her into the hedge on the left but she was having none of it. Our journey mimicked a high speed police chase where the yellow striped car aims to cut of the speeding motorist by swerving in front of it and forcing it to stop! At last the ewe made a sharp right turn in front of us, still running at a fast pace and shot into a driveway to our left.

Joey, Annie's expert sheepdog, was on full alert throughout with his total attention focused on the sheep, nose protruding through the half-open back window behind the driver's seat. With one word from Annie, Joey leapt through the car window and past the ewe steering her into a corner of the garden. He then stood guard, holding her there while Annie manoeuvred the Land Rover as close as we could and Annie rescued the ewe and lifted her into the back. All executed expertly within minutes by awesome Joey, showing yet again the sheep farmer's constant need for a good sheepdog who is able to undertake the wide range of tasks involved in the job.

"Sheep will always escape" a farmer told me once… "the happiest sheep you'll ever see is one who's died in another farmer's field!" he said. He explained that when you really knew sheep you knew that they were always trying to escape and they always thought that 'the grass on the other side of any fence was greener'. Maybe that's why we count sheep.

Talking Tails

Working with Annie I've come to see how relentless is the daily round of foot bathing, injecting, dosing, worming, dagging, ringing, more foot bathing and of course the inevitable moving that goes on when you have a sheep farm, moving large flocks of sheep from this well used field to one with more plentiful lush grazing. Harriet and I have been lucky enough to have the opportunity to take part in all of it ... a whole year of sheep farm activity that either starts or culminates, depending on your viewpoint, with lambing.

We're learning how to collect all two or three hundred sheep into a pen, to guide them, encourage them through the footbath. Harriet is actually now learning that having done all that, when they finally trot out of the foot bath and scatter themselves over the field again... the idea of this job of work is *not* that you run off and round them all up again and drive them back in the pen! To begin with I needed to restrain her until she learned that the activity of gathering and penning and getting them down the run is a job in itself to be praised... job done; incessant regathering and holding them in a pen is not what it's all about. It took a bit of time for her to grasp it and even more to learn to move them forward in the pen at the right pace, encouraging them down the run in single file, neither hassling them nor losing the continual flow, just flanking across the mouth of the pen exerting sufficient authority to keep them steadily moving but not over exciting them

Reluctantly, I have to admit that she is learning her job faster than I'm learning mine; but then she has twice as many legs, ten times more instinct and certainly much more influence over the sheep than I'll ever have. One dog, even a 'not very good dog' is better than any number of humans at getting sheep where you want them… and much more effectively than a quad bike too. Mind you, in the huge fifty or sixty acre fields on Annie's farm it's a wonderful site watching her using her Land Rover and directing both her dogs in opposite directions from the car; whistling to her first dog through the driver window then to the other dog through the passenger window… awesome!

I'm learning about managing the gate on the run to carry out many of the tasks, marking the sheep with different coloured paint sprays identifying all sorts of necessary factors, needs, features… and of course when they're in lamb these markings may indicate whether she is expecting a single lamb or twins with the position of said decoration signifying when the birth is predicted; either early or late in the lambing season. I feel I'm in a paintball game and yes I get splurged aplenty.

Once the dog has been used to get the sheep into the pen they are then encouraged through the funnel at the end of the pen that feeds into an alley way, or race, just wide enough for one sheep. As they run single file up the race they can then be separated by the shedder gate, for example ewes into one pen to the left and their lambs into another on the right.

This run and shedder gate system may be used to divide sheep into different 'cuts' or groups maybe for some treatment or perhaps for market. While I didn't really like the thought of some of the sheep going for slaughter, I recognised the need and also when they've had this 'out to grass' life they have here on Annie's farm it feels okay… I feel similarly alright about eating mutton. Eating lamb is something I haven't wanted or managed to do since becoming this intimate with sheep. I want them to have a full life here on these green fields in the sunshine before they become part of the food chain... to slaughter them too early feels wrong and unnecessary when all I have to do is wait a while.

I've sampled different sheep cheeses since working with sheep too and I've developed quite a taste for them, so it must be that not all sheep farms go in for breeding sheep for slaughter

One of the reasons young lambs may be separated from the ewes is when ringing takes place. I did know about very young male lambs, the wanna-be tups, being castrated with a rubber ring ...but I wasn't prepared for the news that the female lambs too were ringed; all lambs, male and female have their tails ringed. Annie explains that to shorten their tails helps to keep them cleaner which avoids flystrike; keeping their rear ends cleaner makes it easier to 'dag' or shear the rear end fleece during pregnancy. My immediate thought was how awful for the sheep that she'll have no tail to flick away the flies in the heat before I realised of course sheep don't actually use their tails... the only time I've ever seen movement in any tails is from the little lambs as they suckle from the ewe when furious jiggling of the tail would indicate he was attached to the nipple and sucking well.

Following ringing, thereby cutting off the blood supply, the offending body part drops off within days. I read in an old farming book that, on very big farms, these female lambs tails used to be simply cut off and thrown into a bucket to be counted by the farmer at the end of a busy day of cutting and castrating so that he knew the size of his ewe lambing prize ...in other words how many female lambs he had for next year's lambing. Perhaps ringing is a little less gory even if very noisy; each ewe and each lamb bleating until they are all reunited after being separated one side or the other in the run. All quietens down in the field when ewes and lambs, wethers (castrated males) and females, can find each other. I'm assured ringing of either testicles or tails is not too painful on these very young newborne lambs and they don't seem to mind too much... I think I suffer more than they seem to.

Despite my oversensitivity, I have become more involved with the farm work, wanting to do more than just using Harriet to round up the sheep and bring them to the pen. I want to use my hands as well as her, not only to help Annie but try and 'earn' my place and give back something for the time she offers me, but more to participate fully in the farming chores and to piece together the sheep farming year. To this end, I did learn to take part in the ringing of the young lambs as we journey round the fields looking after the labouring and newly delivered ewes. Annie liked the ewe and lamb to have bonded before castration or docking but also she talked to me about the need to ring sheep at under a week old. I had read up on the procedure and asked lots of questions, watched and learned from Annie about how to do it, particularly making sure that the short tail that remained covered both anus and vagina. She then inspected my technique before I was allowed to partake. I'm not sure I'd be able to ring my Herdwicks tails were I ever to own any... I so love seeing their full long tails dangling. The books say it is good husbandry, a health and welfare issue keeping the sheep free from flystrike. I have become almost competent in the task, although I had to discard the rings I dropped on the ground before I became more adept at holding tail, ringing applicator and attaching ring... rather like learning a new medical procedure. Who would have believed I'd find myself doing this in my later life?

* * *

I'm reminded of my first and only spell as a student nurse in theatre, learning to set the various trolleys with the assorted instruments required for each different operation. Each instrument had to be taken from the large, bubbling, steaming, sterilisers; clasping each one with huge Cheatles forceps and steadily transferring each weapon from the boiling water to the trolley.

I had painstakingly prepared one of the trolleys with the instruments in, as I thought, neat orderly rows exactly ready for use for a particular operation from incision to suturing. I looked admiringly at my creation, all beautifully shiny and complete as I covered the surface with a sterile white towel, donned in my own gown, paper hat and mask delivered my creation through the big rubber theatre door into the operations room.

Unfortunately the surgeon, who was notoriously difficult to please, was not left handed (as I am) and when the cover was removed and my handiwork revealed, several expletives emanated as he raised his foot and used his white boot to kick the whole trolley over scattering all the instruments clattering to the marble floor. 'He who shall be obeyed' had spoken.

My time working in theatre was short lived thank goodness… working with unconscious patients was never my forte and I never looked at my best peeking over a mask with perpetually steamed up glasses.

* * *

I manage sheep ringing ok, no problems undertaking that task left handed… and I don't care quite so much about 'looking my best' these days; one of the joys of farm life. Oh, the bliss of getting older and being happy with who you are and less anxious about what others think of you. I'm discovering compensations that come with advancing years, being less obsessed with what you look like is certainly one of them I'd say. Mind you it's an obligatory stance once the inevitable decline creeps on like rust. Stealthily changes sidle in until unexpectedly one day the person who stares back at you from the mirror is your grandmother.

I wonder if my grandmother ever got involved with ringing sheep?

The task of tube feeding a lamb came much more easily as a necessary skill... after all, tube feeding a newborne baby is very similar. I didn't find it too difficult to lay a young lamb on his back across my lap with the neck slightly extended making it really easy to gently navigate a soft rubber tube over the tongue and down the throat guiding it past the windpipe and into the stomach holding the tube to my face to check that no outbreath from the lamb was discernible on my cheek (indicating a misplaced tube). Dripping in a small warm colostrum feed into a fragile lamb who hasn't yet managed to suckle on the ewe is a satisfying thing to accomplish... in fact it took me back to my time on the premature baby unit, little weak bodies in need of warmth and sustenance. Clearly not all my nursing skills are wasted out here on the farm.

* * *

As nurses we not only carried this procedure out on babies but also on adult patients. I remember practising this particular skill on other colleague nursing students during our initial training, trying desperately not to make them gag, or worse still, to throw up. There's probably something to do with health and safety now that would stop all those practise procedures we carried out on each other... but I would agree with the sister tutor who said it helped us to understand what it was like for patients. I will never forget the trauma of having a blanket bath with tepid water where I almost landed on the floor as my colleagues rolled me from side to side as I played the part of an unconscious patient!

Telling Tales

Between us Harriet and I are also learning that herding sheep is a very different task when it involves herding lambs. Many dogs find herding lambs a real challenge and I understand there are some really good working farm dogs who find they can't control lambs. Ewes run more readily through gates, and are more used to doing it but lambs who become separated from their mothers tend to panic. A straggle of lambs can be reluctant to group together. They haven't yet learned to respect the dog and it can be difficult for the dog to steer them through a gate especially when little groups will bunch together to try and make a break for it. This is when even the very good dog can find it impossible to turn back lambs and prevent a mass outbreak. At the moment Harriet looks a bit puzzled by the odd lamb who stands looking at her almost as though he's saying "Hello who are you, have you come to join us?" Then he stands staring at Harriet instead of turning tail and moving off as she believes he should... he hasn't yet learnt to listen to his mother and do what she does when there's a dog around. It's a joy to watch really experienced dogs like Annie's accomplish tasks with lambs.

It is not unusual for a Beardie to bark on occasion while working. I've never heard a border Collie try and move a group by barking but Harriet will occasionally, particularly if a sheep 'stands' to her... she'll first show her teeth and if that doesn't turn him back to the pack, she may bark. Barking at lambs just heightens the panic and can make them run into the fence... more evidence of how much we both have to learn.

I have another activity to add to the list of tasks, that of sheep watching and not only when lambs are in the field. I'm still fascinated by staring at sheep, watching how they play 'follow my leader' or 'how many lambs can we cram together on this little hillock?'

"What is life if full of care and there is no time to stop and stare"

This phrase must have been invented for watching sheep grazing; it's such a tranquil activity it demands you join in and just slow down. Watching a field of Spring lambs gambolling is just enchanting; all running and springing all over the field, climbing on each other and any bucket or bale of hay they can find anywhere. All this skipping around gets their endorphins, their happy hormones, going in their brains along with developing all their muscle and movement.

Then mum notices they are missing and bleating and baaing goes on everywhere with ewes pushing away a lamb that doesn't belong to her while the little fellow looks totally flustered and perplexed, running about in all directions trying to join up while mum then becomes quite desperate when she finds he's the other side of the fence because he's managed to wriggle underneath the gate!

Mis-mothering, where an in-lamb ewe believes a new borne lamb belonging to another ewe is really hers, can happen; again, I understand, it's something that more often occurs with indoor lambing than out in the fields. Driving round the fields with Annie at lambing time it was easy to see why because, with plenty of space, the ewes would take themselves off when labouring, into their own corner either around the edge of the field or between tree roots or tucked into brambles. Closer together in a barn when you're involved in the job of delivering your lamb, it must be easier to wonder if maybe it's already happened and that one nearby, might actually be yours.

I do remember one night on a maternity ward when a new mum rang her bell ... we used to have dim lights over the beds allowing mum to reach and lift her baby from the crib next to her and put him to her breast to feed as soon as he woke without disturbing the rest of the ward. Summoned by her bell I went to see what was happening to find one mum really distressed because she had inadvertently lifted the baby from the cot on her left and begun breast feeding before realising that this wasn't her baby. It was the one from the cot on her right that belonged to her but in her sleepy state and dim lighting a spot of mis-mothering occurred.

There really is something heart-warming about lambs and lambing... an inevitability like the ebb and flow of the tide; as sure as Spring returns each year, so there will be gambolling lambs in green fields with a farm gate to lean on, to stop and stare and give thanks for.

I try to stand and watch at that special early evening time when the magic is triggered and gambolling happens for real. When the lambs all gather and they start playing in earnest, jumping in the air often with all four feet off the ground at once. It's known as 'stotting' and is an action only undertaken by sheep and goats (and gazelles I believe). Then, just as suddenly as it began, it all seems to come to a halt and the hillside returns to its original peaceful grazing place again.

When adult sheep take off 'stotting', all four feet off the ground with three or four consecutive jumps on the trot, it almost looks as though they're about to take flight.

* * *

While lambing as an event often marks the first and inevitable turning of the year's seasons, for me one particular baby's birth has its own place in a well-remembered year, although the rest of the world will remember the date for a very different reason. It was the last delivery I attended before taking time off prior to my own first labour. (Kneeling on the floor trying to get close enough to a delivering mum in the hollow of a big double bed became more difficult the larger my own pregnant abdomen became) She had laboured with her third child on and off for most of the day ... sometimes definitely more 'off' than 'on'. Mum was quite frustrated by seeming to go out of labour again as soon as she called me back. Everything was okay, no problems for mum or babe but labour just seemed to be taking its time to fully establish and begin to apply itself to the job in hand. When she called me for what turned out to be the final time I knew as I drove into the road that things were 'hotting' up because the gate and the front door were open anticipating my arrival. A rather anxious husband met me on the stairs imploring me to hurry up. I was a bit confused as we passed on the stairs, he descended quickly disappearing into the lounge as I headed for the heavy breathing in the bedroom. Indeed the baby's head was just emerging and delivered into my hands while I still had my coat on! I was muttering lots of reassuring noises, while delivering the rest of the baby who loudly announced his arrival. I was just wondering what had happened to Dad, when he entered the bedroom suddenly with his own announcement just as the baby was making his voice heard too ...

"Hurray, we've gone and done it, we really have, we've landed on the moon!" shouted Dad. Mum was just as loud with phrases I have found just as unforgettable but somewhat

unrepeatable here. Evidently, husband considered that Neil Armstrong's accomplishment in being the first man to land on the moon was of greater consequence than the birth of his third child... a view not shared by his wife! Any reference to this notorious 1969 event has me grinning at the memory.

* * *

Yes, events are markers in time and all have their place in history; some more memorable than others, every birth, every lambing. Everything has a place, every event, will leave its mark, big or small, it won't escape being counted.

One lambing birth for the memory bank for me was Itsy. I arrived at the farm one morning, tapped on the back door, let myself into the stone flagged kitchen, and made myself a cup of coffee from the kettle bubbling on the Aga. I waited for Annie to come in from the yard. As she came in she bundled the tiniest scrap into my lap wrapped in a towel. I would never have believed that something so scrawny could make so much noise. Annie had picked him up in the field the previous evening and brought him into the 'nursery' in the barn. He was hypothermic and she wrapped him up and put him under the lamp to try and warm him up but felt sure he wouldn't survive. She was convinced as she did her early morning round that he would have died, he was so tiny and frail. When I tried to stand him, all four limbs spread eagled as I lowered him gently to the floor. He was shouting loudly for food and immediately guzzled from the bottle I offered him, grabbing the teat and sucking ferociously he drained the lot and fell back on my lap. This replete little body was certainly fighting for his life. He just looked too small to survive and Annie warned me that even when these waifs and strays did survive they seldom thrived well; it was as though without their mother's love, and care, life was too hard.

Watching over these motherless ragamuffins… a chorus of them bleating for attention whenever I entered the barn was very special. I think next year I might take up residence in this nursery barn when lambing is at its height. At least I could be useful *and* with the cubicle fences being only a couple of feet high, I can manage to climb over them!

* * *

I'm reminded of my very first Sister post, one of the very few times I returned to hospital nursing for a short while. I was in charge of a children's ward in quite a poor area where we had babies admitted fairly regularly with a diagnosis of 'failure to thrive', coming in for investigations as to the cause. Often undernourished and not gaining weight. I was only in my middle twenties and had no children of my own. This was where I learned about the other meanings attached to the word 'nourishment'. Many times there was no underlying disease or illness; so often these thin underweight tiny bodies had been deprived of more than food coming from homes where they had received little attention, spending long hours alone in a cot with very little human contact and very little if any 'motherly love'. Sometimes parents lacked the ability or the will to devote time and energy into an unwanted baby. Several of these babies were destined to move on to care homes from us. We learned that giving love was every bit as beneficial as a bottle, where to watch a baby learn to respond with a smile was enough to break your heart.

* * *

Here the nursery of orphaned lambs needed to fight to survive without the love of their mum. Itsy survived and I gave him many a bottle before he was big enough to reach the milk bar even when he could support himself on his matchstick legs. The milk bar is a device like a gutter with holes that attach to teats along its base… prepared milk feed can be poured along its length and half a dozen or so hungry lambs all squabble to drink at once before the strongest ones finish it all. I've read that there is an updated model of the milk bar on the market now called 'the shepherdess' where the milk is heated, kept warm and delivered via teats whenever it's needed. Lambs can return as often as they like for a drink, very much as they would feed from mum herself - luxury indeed. Annie thinks it would be a good investment for next year's lambing.

He grew well did Itsy; in fact he always looked out of proportion, long spindly legs and a fat belly. In time he went out on the hill with all the others and for me there was always an extra bit of pleasure watching him head off happily gambolling with the other lambs. There was something almost biblical in pretending I was a shepherd who had taken part in 'finding', (well 'saving' in Itsy's case), the lost sheep! I had a soft spot for him and, on the day the fattest ones from that flock were going to be drawn for slaughter, I chose not to work the shedder-gate. He'd had an eventful life and I felt I knew him. I wanted him to stay and munch fresh green grass for ever, he'd fought hard to live.

I'm sure part of the secret of farming well and efficiently has to be not getting emotionally involved with your stock… I'm not sure I'd manage that. I think all those poorly, hand reared ones might have names if they belonged to me and if I'd watched them struggle to make it through, how would I then just shedder-gate them into the pen, on to the trailer and off to the market? I guess there will be many more Itsys… and I'll probably get attached to all of them.

You made your mark Itsy, your life counted; you were the first lamb I helped to hand rear.

Today another 'saving' story that I think will stay in the memory bank happened today; one that will leave its mark on several young lives I suspect... not a world shattering event but a bit special.

I always like our Land Rover journey into the fields along by the river, and never more so than at lambing time. Occasionally we've downed a cup of coffee from our flask sitting on the embankment here while on our rounds. When the pressure of inspecting all the sheep in all the fields is not too full-on, perhaps after shearing, and when dogs have worked well and sheep have decided they'll behave and not cause trouble, we might savour the odd sunny day, disembark and take a break sitting around the base of one of the large trees where its lower branches reach down into the river.

Never at lambing time though, life is too hectic. However, as we turn off the road and head across the field to drive along the track running along the embankment, there is a small excited group of young lads jostling each other to get a better view of some action happening in the river. As we approach two or three of them ran towards us all chattering over one another. Annie called to me as she got out, to come quickly and bring a towel. When I approached, the leader of the boys was staggering out of the river (water well above his knees) coming up the bank holding a new born lamb! Apparently the group had seen the lamb stagger to his feet after quietly watching the birth from a few yards away on the footpath. They had been totally involved in the magic of it all when, just as they began to walk on, one of the lads turned back and noticed the lamb had disappeared. The party headed back to see that the lamb had tumbled down the bank into the water and was now floating out to the centre of the river. The leader had then clambered down and rescued him. It turned out to be a small group of inner city youngsters coming out into the country on a nature walk. We took the lamb and wrapped him in the towel while Annie explained that we'd take him and the ewe back to the barn to warm him up and pen them together to help them bond.

The leader was emptying river water out of his boots assuring us that he'd dry out OK on the train as they returned to London! We left with the ewe and two dogs in the back of the Land Rover and a rather bedraggled lamb wrapped up on my lap.

* * *

As we drove off I thought back to my own school trips and could only recall a dreary visit to a sewage works where we were made to drink a glass of water at the end. This wonderfully informative visit was supposed to open our eyes to modern development methods that brought sewage in at one end of the plant and cleverly converted the filth to clean water fit to drink at the other extremity of the building. I think I might have found watching a lamb born and rescuing it rather more scintillating.

* * *

I hope the kids were still chatting about what they'd seen and would hold on to the excitement they had felt in their memory banks for ever.

The Cast Sheep

Another word in the shepherding vernacular I had heard but was unsure of the meaning when applied to sheep was 'cast'. I think I did know at the back of my mind that somehow when sheep got over onto their backs they were in danger of not being able to right themselves to standing. But I had never seen or experienced what can happen to these 'cast' sheep. A sheep stuck in this position, a situation from which they are totally unable to escape unaided, may be because of a wet or heavy fleece. It possibly occurs more often with broad back mountain breeds of sheep.

Previously I had only known about plaster casts… certainly immovable objects that require some assistance to escape from!

I saw today just how traumatic and perilous it can be for a ewe heavy in lamb to get into this cast position. As we drove into one of the fields Annie was looking over to the far side of a large field concentrating her gaze at the base of the hill where there was a slight dip. I could see she was concerned as she closed the gate behind the Land Rover and then sped straight across in the direction of the large white bulk with the occasional flailing legs clearly visible. Several large crows were circling above her helpless body and frequently, one after the other, they were diving down into the middle of the mayhem, ominously indicating all was not well.

As we drove alongside, the sight we had been dreading was revealed, two dead new borne lambs still wet. With no mum to lick them dry and safeguard them from their assailants, they were fated. Wedged as she was, unable to get to her feet she had been powerless to protect her lambs from the murderers. With no first feed of the life-sustaining colostrum, with no-one to defend them, her young had both been attacked and slaughtered by these circling savage killers. Evidence of attack to both the umbilicus and the eyes of each lamb displayed before us.

Between us we rolled the ewe over and lifted her back onto her feet; she was weak and unsteady, and had clearly been cast for several hours. Annie decided we should bring her back to the barn for some warmth and TLC (tender loving care) for a while to help her recover; we loaded her aboard. Annie then bundled the afterbirth into a plastic carrier bag and as she jumped into the Land Rover said she had an idea she was going to try.

Words tumbled over one another as we bumped over the field and along the back lane and into the farmyard. Annie explained that a very short while ago, just before I arrived at the farm today, on her first early morning inspection of the first of the lambing fields, she had rescued a lamb, the second of twins where the ewe had abandoned the little fellow. Believing she had completed her job having the first twin and suckling that one immediately, she had steadfastly disowned the second, smaller one, butting him away whenever he attempted to nurse.

Annie had returned with him to the nursery barn and had him warming up under the lamp bleating loudly for his mum. She went on to say that as the 'cast' ewe we had just rescued had been unable to lick and mother-up her now dead lambs, there was a chance of 'gifting' her this abandoned lamb. There was only a chance and probably only an outside chance Annie stressed because many times these attempted adoptions were unsuccessful but as she lifted the little disowned lamb from under the lamp, she doused him with the afterbirth fluids from the cast ewe, as I was settling her into a makeshift pen within the nursery that we hastily erected from a few hurdles. She was steadying up on her feet and I distributed some straw around as Annie placed our forsaken lamb next to her in the pen. She leant gently into the ewe and checked her udder... it was full and as Annie squeezed the teat, the milk began flow. We both stood quietly by the pen as the ewe bowed down and began to nuzzle 'her' lamb. We held our breath as she began to lick him dry, protecting him from chilling, making him her own. She was making murmuring noises like those I'd heard before from contented ewes as their young began to feed. The baaing from the discarded lamb began to subside as it nudged its way in beneath the ewe searching for the teat. As his tail began to jiggle and we listened, the sucking could clearly be heard as this hungry chap was definitely not going to miss out on this opportunity of warm colostrum... he'd waited long enough! This wet adoption seemed destined to work. It was a special miracle of nature unfolding, watching this forsaken lamb feed, seeing his belly round beneath him, was indeed a memory to be treasured.

To witness the maternal instincts strengthen as she gave undivided attention to this unintended 'off spring' was so good... the stakes were high... to almost feel his chances of survival multiply when so recently his life had hung by a thread was humbling and unforgettable.

* * *

I felt a shudder run over me as I remembered the absolute wonder I felt as I shared my first delivery as a young midwife, sharing the intimacy of the experience with the family, listening to that first cry, watching as he latched onto the breast for the first time. I wondered whether everyone felt like this... would all my deliveries be this wondrous, this unforgettable? Yes, by and large, they were; full of emotion matched only in intensity by the sadness suffered when there is no first breath or where very short lives were cruelly snatched away despite all efforts ... where depths of grief so exhaustive, drowned all and any other emotion.

Magic Moments

On my way to the farm and Annie today and, as usual, I'm nearly as excited as Harriet. I'm murmuring a thank you to Harriet on the back seat, thanking her for all she has brought to my retired life

Many of us dog owners have a very special relationship with our dog, the strength and substance of which defies both understanding and explanation to anyone who hasn't been similarly afflicted. It's something more than an extreme sense of companionship; it's about the two of you knowing each other in a way that's incomprehensible to anyone outside the union. The connection is hidden within a shared life experience built on disposition, attention and love. It doesn't depend on the dog's intrinsic worth or potential but rather the coming together of kindred spirits in partnership. Few of us own up to the depth of such a relationship, probably due to the discomfiture that hovers close to the confession. Inherent in any relationship that reaches this depth, is an exchange of devotion, and the pet dog lovers amongst us know that this adoration is not simply from dog to master, but from human to hound in equal measure.

Harriet has been responsible for all this new avenue of interest, right from her attraction to sheep through to many a cold, wet, muddy field, attendance at sheep herding clinics and trials.

She sits up on the back seat and begins to whine as I turn off the highway and head out towards the farm; I'll never know how she can register where we're going when we're still a mile or so away.

I find myself talking to Harriet while we car travel in much the same way as I chat to her when we walk unaccompanied... many friends have admitted to similar behaviour.

There is a huge reward that comes from undertaking the regular pilgrimage of dog walking alone. We allow ourselves to think of our dogs as friends. Along with the 'dog - friend', a type of harmless amnesia creeps in and enables us to escape our ordinary lives. The solitary walk is an aid to creativity when the head is too full of everything; settling into the rhythm of the walk shakes ideas into a shape that makes sense, that enables suspension of disbelief while holding on to a wide range of possibilities. There is often the awakening of an inspired something that might just banish last night's writer's block, while at the same time, finding the private dog walk to be incredibly meditative... even mindful. While much of my social life is often focused around walking the dog, sometimes the solitary pilgrimage just reaps rewards.

The Changing Seasons

I've been reflecting on how much I love farm life where the seasons seem to hold so much more meaning than simple dates on a calendar. The bedrock of the why when and how of the farmer's workload is defined by the changing seasons, the fundamentals of need so different from those of the city dweller. Country life reflects the long hours needed to keep pace with all weathers, leading to a lack of pretence about how life really works. This results in a somewhat harder life than the image perceived by the summer day visitor. There is a truth here where, in many ways, endurance and resilience replace romanticism.

I've always felt most 'at home' in the countryside and have remembered back with a quiet longing to stand again in the cowslip filled field behind my childhood home. Tall stems with yellow flowers escaping from the buds attaching them to the stalk. I would pick bunches of them to take home. It's my earliest memory of being alone and loving it, believing it was my field. It belonged just to me.

Much of my childhood seems to have been spent around the village pond and playing in the fields by the River Misbourne. Moving to London in 1960 to train for nursing was the first big change from village life. These were unforgettable years and looking back now it was clearly a time (or perhaps season) of change for many.

Despite the excitement of leaving home and experiencing those changes through the 60s in the big city, I remember the anticipation whenever I steamed out of Marylebone station heading for home on days off; watching the buildings becoming more scattered with each clickety clack as the sprawling countryside alongside the railway track became more pronounced with the green landscape intensifying with every station.

When I lived as a 'townee' the changing of the seasons seemed somehow less immediately apparent, and in no way was my pattern of work defined by the weather. Blue skies or grey, rain or shine, shorter days or longer nights, travelling by bike or car, the work schedule remained constant.

I am much more aware on the farm of the need to take account of the weather; not only the extra attention needed when lambing is cold and snowy but the dry days needed for shearing, taking care to get things done before the daylight fades… and what of all those crops? I'm now beginning to appreciate how work hours and probably income are determined by both the seasons and the weather. Moreover, it seems that if you work with the land, you need to be prepared for the hand that mother-nature deals you within each season change; a long hot summer, a drought, unprecedented torrential rain…

* * *

As I moved to various southern county locations during my years of district nursing practice, moments to enjoy the countryside have managed to squeeze themselves into my life, very often between patient visits. I would often choose the route between one house and another that would take me past a buttercup field or alongside a row of autumnal trees… these small communes with nature never failed to lift my spirits and many of my memorable times from various places are hooked around these seasonal settings.

Harriet of course led me into all those country walks on my retirement… finally leading me here onto the farm I'm so growing to love…. a dog for all seasons!

Where to begin a farming year? Many maintain that it's the Spring and lambing that heralds the start of the year and certainly the cold and mud of winter with its dark mornings and nothing growing, could be seen as the end of things. But others would consider Autumn and tupping as the true start, the real beginning of the farming year.

As the warmth of September melts away, it gives way to October with its chilly mornings bringing the first forebodings of winter. The thistle is still managing to produce new amythyst flowers around the edges of the fields while the hawthorn berries are darkening to a deeper ruby red. The elderberry has finished and only the lacy filigree stalks remain, waving above the bushes. The conkers and acorns still scattered on the floor near the fences are looking withered and sunken.

The days shorten accompanied by a weak, low lying sun before the night frosts set in leading to that crunch underfoot in the early mornings. The shorter days with the loss of daylight affects the hormones bringing the ewes into season which lasts five weeks. Putting the rams in with the ewes now… tupping, is the usual time to ensure there will be lambs in the spring.

There are a few hard frosts in late November and early December when the grass is starched and glistening under my boots and when in the absence of snow the frost is thick enough to make the sheep coats look positively grubby

The grey skies of the early months of this year form a dreary backdrop for the skeletal framework of the winter trees. Even when the clocks go forward the bitter cold seems determined to hold back Spring, indulging instead in wind, snow flurries, driving sleet and mud. Every gateway on the farm seems to get deeper in mire at every visit

With all of the disordered weather this year, very few early catkins and snowdrops brave the elements but the bright sulphur yellow of the coltsfoot braves it on one of the few sunny days in early March. There are remnants of the bracken scattered around at the field edges making a rusty fringe along by some of the electric fencing.

The hedgerows begin to bud and then are scattered with splashes of white May flowers though we're still only in April avoiding the showers with some very cold mornings. Those same hawthorn hedges become thick with blossom as we go through May giving me their own special welcome as I drive into the farmyard. I remember as a child being told we weren't to pick these hawthorn flowers as it was considered unlucky to bring them in doors. Grey wagtails are in residence up under the low barn roof and as I park the car, if I stand up on the bank I can see her sitting on her clutch of buff coloured eggs under the roof.

The cow parsley is everywhere like huge enormous waves around the woody edges of the fields; Harriet crashes through them and comes out adorned with their tiny white flowers, shakes herself vigorously and almost as much lands on her again before she moves on.

Baby lambs nestled amongst early daffodils looking exactly as they should for any Easter card, their mother grazing next to the fluffy pussy willow nearby. The elderflower bushes reach high and just show the beginning of flower heads, but somehow don't seem quite to be able to complete the job.

Mid May and the shiny dark green leaves of the bluebells begin to push up through the woodland floors surrounding some of the fields confirming the journey into spring with a few more chilly frosts reminding us that she's just having trouble waking up this year.

The trees are slower to show their green wardrobe. The bright fresh almost transparent leaves of the beech begin to unfurl.

May is the time to reflect on how the oak and ash have fared this year, are we in for a dry or rainy summer?

During April the black and brown buds of the oak and the ash can usually be seen competing for who will make it first. Sadly, the ash are so few now following the ash dieback disease that has affected so many of the younger ones. Some of the older ones are still hanging on. I'm hoping the oak will win out...

> 'oak before ash the summer's a splash,
> ash before oak in for a soak'.

We surely must have had our 'soak' already this year, evidenced by the muddy gateways suffered by the early March lambs.

The intensive mothering displayed by those early delivering ewes was a real lesson in mothering. So often she had carefully chosen her birthing place either tucked in between a few bushes or protected from the biting winds behind a heap of turnips, even a large hollowed out tree trunk. Watching them licking their lambs dry, sometimes described as the elixir of life, listening to the gentle murmuring baas as she bonds with her young lamb or lambs is magic every time, nudging them, encouraging them to their feet while she stands waiting for them to suckle. The protection gained from this good first colostrum feed not only sustains the lamb against the bitter weather but also gives resistance to possible infection in the early days.

So often viewing these captivating early encounters emphasises for me just how incapable the human baby is for such a long time compared with the lamb... struggling to its feet, fighting for a feed and coping with inclement conditions within minutes of birth and within days sturdily making its place in the world…. the ewe protecting him and maybe his twin sister against predators through long cold days and nights.

Our human mothering, it would seem, is somewhat less demanding requiring only feeding with judicious nappy changing and a few weeks of broken nights; how fortunate are we? The uncontrolled mischievous toddler may perhaps impersonate the skipping lamb I suppose but then not many toddlers get their head stuck in the fence while mum's munching lunch.

The plus must be that the ewe doesn't have stroppy teenagers to contend with, so human mothering is not all blessed!

Summertime comes and there seems little time between lambing and shearing. This is when the farmer wants long hot summer days with dry sheep to be able to push on with herding and penning the sheep ready for the shearers; a long tiring job when both shepherd and sheep dispense with their outer garments. Those elderflower bushes are now fully clothed in all their glory… elderflower abundance ready for me to harvest and make a thirst quenching cordial.

Arable ground looks at its best in the summer with fields of tall hay and growing cereals. The look of a green landscape punctuated with brash yellow rapeseed fields must surely attract any would-be artist to attempt to capture this now commonplace spectacle.

I really like the mix of cattle, sheep and growing foodstuffs on Annie and Dan's farm. There's a wholesome feel about it, both animal and plant life growing together; a feeling probably engendered by a totally unrealistic desire to live the self-sufficient lifestyle with Barbara and Tom in 'The Good Life' where I could have my Herdwick sheep and claim grazing rights on the village green. The nearest we get to that is when Harriet and I are driving a few hundred sheep along country lanes and over growing turnip fields to a new grazing site.

These turnips will eventually be used for sheep to gorge on but, while they are not yet ready for harvesting, the sheep need encouraging to stay on track and not separate off from the pack and begin foraging. Harriet flanks back and forth keeping the whole flock moving forward... as a droving dog, this is her forte. She settles in well behind concentrating on the task in hand showing her teeth to any ewe who decides to challenge her authority and stray off the path. I don't blame the sheep really, the tiny lush green turnip tops are beginning to look quite delicious and I should think they make a tasty change from grass.

Wild roses and fragrant honeysuckles transform the hedgerows while wildflowers are dotted among the grasses, some large and shouting, some fragile and quiet but all pleasing to the eye. This year I find myself waiting for a huge long bank of bright, deep-pink foxgloves that flowed along one valley at the side of a bridleway we scurried past in the Land Rover last year on our way to footbath some sheep... a magnificent display I've been holding in my memory hoping it will be repeated; there was such a huge number that there surely must have been enough to give us a goodly exhibit again even allowing for their bi-annual propensity.

This year at Annie's is turning out to be a little different than the usual expected English summer. Really through the last half of June and all of July, we've experienced a really prolonged dry spell; an unaccustomed excessively dry summer. I can't quite believe how dry and brown it all looks; rolling biscuit-coloured hills rising around us wherever we're working. The once lush green sheep-grazing fields seem covered with spikey, tall, straw-like grass and Harriet has to leap above it as she strives to see and reach the sheep. It seems to make it more difficult for her to hear my commands and whistles too. I've taken to coming to the farm really early so it's cooler to work the sheep who are wanting to retreat and rest in the shade. Traveling early is great, reminiscent of setting off on holiday with the children... no traffic, Harriet and I excited and we arrive in the farmyard to a hum of activity while the rest of the world it seems are still abed. So good to make the most of it, after about 10.30am it all becomes unbearably hot until about 10 o'clock in the evening when the temperature drops to a comfortable level. Harriet heads for the trough once she's worked and lies down in it, seeming to like the water on her belly while she drinks.

As I drive I see whole fields full of bales of hay and straw, showing themselves off in the early morning sun, evidence of the hard work undertaken by Dan and the other farmers. I can't quite believe how brown and dusty the landscape is, a hotter, dryer summer that has been more intense and humid than I remember. I haven't noticed the silage making either, the sweet smell of cut grass as it pickles already wrapped. Winter feed for both the sheep and cattle are having to be used now because of the lack of grass for grazing.

Right at the end of August there are a few splashes of rain. The temperature drops nicely but really we need a heavier downfall for the grass to grow and for those baby turnips to flourish.

The unprecedented hot spell has brought blackberries into fruit early, but even they look as though they'd like a good drink to fatten themselves up and become fully juicy. The elderberries hang heavily from the boughs and seem to make the absolute most of any small shower.

* * *

Just to see them takes me back to the red-tiled larder floor in my childhood home with the large stone casks of fermenting elderberry wine my mother treasured. I can almost hear the sound of exploding corks in the night from the most recently-filled wine bottles.

* * *

The long hot spell comes to an end and the rain finally comes as September, and its flaming colours and mellow fruitfulness, merge with the lengthening shadows as the nights draw in heralding the reiteration of the farming year. The bright red hips on the wild rose bushes announce the arrival of Autumn.

With all the long, hard hours the farmer works I wonder why so few of them give up farming and opt for an easier way of life. Many have needed to diversify and have found innovative ways of raising more money… often not so dependent on the weather. Barns have been converted into self-catering holiday homes and farmhouse rooms let out for bed and breakfast. I was even lucky enough when on holiday in Cornwall, to spot a notice at the end of a farm drive advertising a chance to sit on a hay bale eating a clotted cream scone while he, the farmer, showed us all what his sheepdogs could do… great entertainment for a small entrance fee. But with increasing need for more income, he stays working the land in one way or another, animal or arable.

I suspect it is more about the way of life rather than the income that holds the farmer to his trade, but maybe it's more to do with the value he's able to put on a beautiful sunrise or sunset, the magic of the first primrose bank in full bloom or maybe the smell of honeysuckle on a warm summer evening. Does job satisfaction come simply from getting a good price for his sheep, or does he see value in watching and listening to a ewe with her new borne lamb. Are these the things that make the job worthwhile for him or is it simply my sentimentality that wants it to be so? Is it these magic moments that bring worth and fulfilment into the job of farming?

* * *

I struggled at times in my nursing career to explain the payback for the long hours and low salary; what it was about care that fed my soul; that made going to work a privilege rather than a chore. By the time I retired, the layers of management had worked hard at destroying that pay-back, at taking away the job satisfaction that comes from therapeutic nursing. Instead they had elevated the importance of computer tasks and targets over and above hands-on quality patient care. The name of the game seemed to be to reduce nursing staff numbers and expand each caseload with the resultant loss of quality care and carer pay-back

* * *

Maybe farmers like Annie and Dan have managed to hang on to that payback. Maybe by holding on to a way of life where because the elements, the seasons, allow less control over what life chooses to deliver, there is an acceptance, a resilience to what comes their way. Somehow they are able to endlessly measure the ups and downs of everyday life against what remains meaningful and appreciated. Is it the stillness of a warm summer evening or the accompaniment of the dawn chorus on that early check of the lambing fields that feeds the spirit... even when your sheep fail to sell at market or the price paid for wool doesn't cover the cost of shearing?

Undeniably, there was a time when life was slower that encouraged the awareness of now and what it meant, rather than this pushing ever faster trying to stuff even more into the next five minutes of living. Looking back to a time when the pace of life was slower is something I find myself doing more these days… not with a longing to put back the clock… more a desire to take more time doing or looking at or 'being in' what's happening here and now with less hurry. Not bemoaning the fact that a loaf of bread now costs ten shillings in old money (goodness, echoes of mum's words), more about giving ourselves time to talk, to listen, to laugh and to cry without this incessant rush on to the next thing. It appears the world is spinning forward while I'm continually falling behind it would seem.

* * *

Just occasionally glancing over my shoulder to a slower, gentler way of life makes me wonder whether that's something else we've thrown away… just like the caring art that I believe was demonstrated in so many ways in district nursing as we knew it. A time when I served the community of patients I lived amongst, giving care rather than constantly chasing and recording facts, figures and management targets.

* * *

Another of mum's sayings I've learned to cherish in later years, "There's all day tomorrow not touched yet", a much softer feel that I've adopted in retirement rather than "Don't put off 'till tomorrow what you can possibly do today" I might just buy a fridge magnet I saw the other day that said 'Don't let's die of improvement'. Am I just getting lazy with advancing years or can I twist it around and talk about being wiser as I grow older with an awareness of the good things in this very moment being too precious to miss by filling life with busyness?

I have to acknowledge the contribution Harriet has made to all this contemplation; so many of the seeds of my reflections were sewn during my more solitary dog walks... reflections on my life along with an appreciation of where I am now is borne out of time spent with Harriet.

At the end of many a solitary walk I have highly improbable plans on how Harriet and I can become shepherd and sheepdog on our own farm, where we keep sheep and make our own sheep's cheese that tastes every bit as good as Manchego (a Spanish ewes' cheese) which has its own exclusive label and becomes known throughout the land as a 'must have' staple for any cheese connoisseur! One of the inexplicable phenomena when walking is that, if you are accompanied by a dog, you can talk to anyone and anyone can talk to you – about anything. Many pipedreams and fantasies have been shared with dog walking friends... many of whom would admit to knowing only your dog's name however effusive is their greeting when you meet.

* * *

Long before I ever owned a dog, when I was working as a district midwife in the wilds of Sussex, one morning I became aware of the obligatory change that happens to anyone walking a dog, giving them the ability to talk to anyone they see... maybe it is the escapee element of the dog walker as they commune with nature rambling in the countryside in the early hours. I had been most of the night attending a birth in a rural hamlet and left to return home just as dawn was deciding to break on, what promised to be, a glorious summer morning. The slate grey night sky was lightening slowly edged with a glow as dawn was breaking. I was merrily riding my bike with the delivery accoutrements on the back, looking forward to breakfast and bed. It was a route I knew well and as I rode down the hill I lifted my legs out each side as I was about to splash through the ford as it crossed the road at the bottom.

A little black dog began to run alongside me in the half-light barking as he tried to keep up with me. These were the days when dogs ran around outside unaccompanied, coming and going as they pleased, returning home when they were hungry. Believing us to be on our own, I heard myself singing out "Good morning little dog running along by the hedge" ... and then tumbling off my bike as I heard a male voice from the other side of the hedge say "Good morning lady on a bicycle!"

Buster was the first dog I came to know, well properly, when, shortly after this, I cared for his owner at home following a hospital stay... he was so loyal to his owner, I think that's where my longing to have a dog began. Who would have thought it would be five decades later and a sheepdog?

The Return of the Clinic

Harriet and I headed off to a whole three days of our first sheepherding clinic this year... even at 6am I am light of heart. The sun is coming up and Harriet settles down on the back seat ready for the journey. There's a sense of anticipation about her when we set off early; bags in the car, wellies and rainwear hanging on back of seat. It looks as though it might be a 'good-weather-day', but one thing I've learned about playing with sheep is that wet and cold weather clothing need to accompany us on every single occasion whatever the forecast says. Even the 'Queue Ahead : 40 miles an hour' sign as I join the M25 is insufficient to dampen my enthusiasm and as I settle in for a slow journey. I fast-forward in thought to when I'll be f coming off the field later on and making my way down the country lanes to the dog friendly pub for the night.

The farm we all meet at to practise our herding is in a hamlet that consists of little more than the farm itself and within a couple of miles an Inn that I'm particularly fond of. Harriet is not just welcomed in the bar but also allowed in my bedroom. Just returning there at the end of a tiring day and soaking in a hot bath while reflecting on the day's performance cannot be bettered... well the large glass of red wine that follows hopefully restores hope that maybe tomorrow I might manage to recover from the less than perfect execution of the shedding manoeuvre we attempted today. Harriet always steadfastly refuses to join in with my reflective thought discussions on 'what went wrong today'... she of course knows any mistakes were definitely nothing to do with her and are only ever down to the considerable lack of expertise on the part of her owner.

But today we arrive on the field on time and fortuitously just in time to watch the master himself putting one of his young dogs through his paces. I try to encourage Harriet to watch, a totally wasted attempt, while I become transfixed by the seemingly effortless way that the dog took the sheep through gates and along the cross drive with such precision following the most unobtrusive whistle commands. Harriet just tramples excitedly around my feet with a definite look of "Let me get to it, I can do much better" Regrettably Harriet, nothing could be farther from the truth.

I'm thinking about the trainer's words when he tells me to have confidence in her; so often Harriet behaves as though confidence is the one thing she's definitely *not* lacking... it's the ability to go with it I'm not so sure of. Maybe it's her defensive front that leads her to behave in such a self-assured way. I gaze down at her little upturned face looking up at me with her ears pricked up all ready to go; maybe she senses my own lack of confidence and is determinedly attempting to drag me along in her wake. It's sometimes scary how closely she appears to read my thoughts. I realise she can't actually be doing that but I'm at a loss to know what else it is, what movements I make or facial expressions I display that enable her to translate my mood or intended action so accurately.

She really does appear to read my mind at times, not so much on the field as in everyday life, I'll think about doing something or going in some particular direction and she sets off that way, as though I've actually said it out loud. Sometimes it's uncanny and makes me wonder what untapped abilities our pet dogs have that we haven't even recognised, let alone harnessed. I'm unable to make an adequate assessment of what this dog has brought into my life; the scope and depth of her gifts are too huge to quantify.

The Championship

I feel embarrassed to mention the word but then it's an episode that should be recorded because, looking back on the event, it marked how the tables had turned for me, when it became clear that it really was doing the farm work, developing a working dog on the farm, that meant so much more than the trialling.

Somehow it feels it should have been something so different that flowed here underneath such a title… 'the championship' should offer so much more than the actual outcome.

Harriet and I had taken part in a small trial down in Kent where we had run in trials before, so we both knew the field. It was a small field which was good for those of us with inexperienced dogs or where experienced handlers could begin to run their young dogs they were beginning to train. It was a wild day with wind and rain seeming to come across in all directions. Many of the competitors were facing a lot of trouble getting the sheep down the field at all, most seemed to have sheep running back to try to join the other sheep in the let out pen. I watched thinking "Oh Harriet should be able to manage that bit; I'm sure she'll get them down to me". Indeed she did, even though it wasn't very pretty and we didn't achieve too much after that, missing gates on the drive and being timed out before the shed. So it was a real surprise to find that we were presented with a rosette for second place at the end of the trial. If I tell you the marks… first place got 87 and we got 43, the difference in ability of the handlers is there for all to see! We 'won' the place purely because the weather had kept many competitors away and secondly so many runners had to retire with their dogs unable to lift and fetch the sheep down to the handler. Regardless of these mitigating circumstances I remained overjoyed with our achievement; reality played no part in my exaggerated excitement… well not until…

On the strength of this laughable achievement, I was shaken to discover that the first two competitors, Mr 87 points and me, Mrs shouldn't-really-be-here, would now go forward to the area championship! I was aghast and felt sure this couldn't happen but was told that this was the first time this club had been offered the opportunity to enter the championship and it would be letting the club down if we didn't accept. First and second places were required to attend.

With a heavy heart I agreed and when the big day came spent I the entire morning petrified' To be amongst all these tried and trusted dogs and handlers, me wanting to stay and hide in the car, knowing this was all well beyond both of us, me believing it must be some ghastly joke… The dreaded time arrived and we walked to the post. Neither of us had ever seen an outrun this long before. A friendly voice was reminding me that there was no pen here, we were to drive the sheep up into the trailer over there to finish the course. I did manage to stutter that should we get that far on the course I might need picking up from the ground following a dead faint. The judge did grin and wish me luck.

This is where I really want to be able to describe the fantastic run that had the whole field cheering with me walking proudly behind the sheep with my dog as we drove them to the exhaust pen. Sadly, it was not to be… my greatest hope was that Harriet would make a good attempt at the outrun, maybe lift, if I was really lucky, and I would need to take the long walk of shame to help her take the sheep off.

Harriet stood firmly on my left hand side and refused to move. Despite whistles, commands, repeated commands, encouraging arm movements all to no avail... I think I might even have jumped up and down on the spot as did Harriet, barking loudly. As we sloped back to the car, both with our tails between our legs, I smiled as I recalled the phrase "Rome wasn't built in a day". A well-known competitor who had been a part of the national and international sheepdog trials many times followed me off the field. I felt his hand on my shoulder as he added kindly "the first thousand trials are the worst!" I managed a smile...

This was to be the one and only championship we were ever to come near; certainly nothing to write home about as they say, but with all of that disappointment and gut wrenching embarrassment, my pleasure and satisfaction at working with Harriet on the farm continues to grow and, dare I say, improve. It's as though I'm in the wrong group of outsiders ... I'm not a weekend hobby triallist, I'm a hobby shepherd; I'm trying to get into what many farmers are good at already while they are wanting to move on and learn to trial their farm dogs.

I want a sheep farm... they want to compete and win trophies!

Changes Afoot

Looking at where I am in my part-time shepherding retirement life on the farm, I've become more aware of how much change has happened in farming in my lifetime and how changes continue to impact on the daily life of the farmer and indeed on the life of the working sheepdog.

I remember the fields around my village always seeming to be full of sheep as we walked the footpaths to school; not so now... but then the decline in the number of green fields has been continuous it seems. I remember walking those footpaths as wartime prefabs came down and houses went up in the surrounding fields and the sheep disappeared. The haystacks I had played in as a child are long gone, replaced by large black plastic covered bales. I remember visiting patients as a district nurse and midwife in tied cottages across farms, each inhabited by the many farm workers employed there... a lifestyle seldom seen now.

I have read that the wholesale clearing of these estate cottages has now been halted and the derelict houses have been sold to owners who want to renovate them. Perhaps this could be seen as a revival of village life maybe?

Sometimes when I go to other farms watching trials I really like to look at the surrounding landscape especially when it is undulating or craggy and wonder who lived on it many years ago, who were they and how did they make a living from it, were the fields cultivated then or were their sheep 'hefted' on this patch of moorland? If there's a farm standing high above the green fertile land below, do those hills maybe get snow early, even if only a dusting. I drove back over Dartmoor with Annie after some training and we drove through a blizzard sweeping across gorse and heather either side of the high road with scattered sheep and distant dilapidated outbuildings. Did someone manage a farm here, were they able to eke out a living with their sheep even as recently as my childhood perhaps, post war in the fifties although there was no sign of any active farm or sheep now. What changes has farm life seen here? The snow was nowhere to be seen as we came off the moor.

It seems sheep have been looked after in much the same way over time with one of the earliest ways of sheep farming involving driving sheep from the lowlands up into the hills once the snow had melted and then back down to those lowlands for summer grazing on grass, fodder and turnips. History reveals wool production from sheep was established way before the industrial revolution, it being one of the main sources of wealth for Britain at that time. Large scale sheep farming formed much of our landscape with wool production as an industry increasing through medieval times. 'Baa Baa Black Sheep' is thought to be the oldest nursery rhyme, referring to bags of wool being counted.

Now it seems farmers are out of pocket after shearing, other manmade fibres being preferred.

While the tractor and combine harvester have taken over from the horse, there are many who are at a loss to understand why anyone would choose a quad bike over a real live Collie to work their sheep. However, there are other changes that affect how, when and where the sheepdog works and why his role is changing too. It seems that motorised shepherding will be at least part of how the shepherd manages his flock in all but the most mountainous terrain. Therefore, it could happen that the sheepdog is used only when working close at hand with sheep.

Farmers often used to choose hardy mountain ewes, but now tend to go for larger breeds of lowland sheep. These changes, together with indoor lambing, are becoming more common place and, as such, maybe what we need our sheepdogs for is changing.

Listening to farmers talk I've heard discussions about this or that dog being more of a trialling dog than a working farm dog... and many of the good sheepdog triallists seem to use their 'trial dogs' less for farm work, putting more time and effort into training the dog solely for trialling. So it could be suggested that the sport of trialling has also changed and moved a long way from where it started, with local farmers putting their dogs through their paces, mimicking the farm work done by their sheepdogs, competing in a game of rivalry with other farmers.

So, despite the possibility of less farm work for the sheepdog, and potentially more people outside the world of farming becoming more interested in the sport, will there be sheepdogs bred purely for trialling? Indeed, is that happening now... dogs bred for trials with maybe a lack of the stamina required for everyday heavy flock work? Listening to those discussions at trials about who bred whom, while also considering the tolerance of hobby triallists, it perhaps has to be deemed a serious possibility or even eventuality.

A recent article in the I.S.D.S (International Sheep Dog Society) magazine discussed the practice of now breeding the Border Collies only for trialling, with the suggestion that some of these are 'soft' dogs unable to carry out a full working day on the farm.

I laugh now as I think of myself in this hobby or weekend triallist group because now I know that really my love (and dare I say Harriet's love) is actually partaking in all the everyday work on the farm, something she enjoys so much more than the trialling game.

I'm remembering a lovely day in the early summer before the drought, when, in the middle of a mornings work with the sheep up in the hills, Annie parked the Land Rover in a field with a magnificent view overlooking a large flock of sheep and produced a basket with coffee and biscuits. As we sat on the grass soaking up not just the sun... but for me the whole ambience of where I was and what I was so fortunate to be doing, when Annie took a photo of Harriet on her phone. Harriet was so clearly waiting to work, to be a *farm* dog... here we are working sheepdog and shepherd enjoying farm life.

This is where I am with a 'make' of dog that used to be a working sheep dog but has long since been out of favour and fashion for shepherding and certainly is rarely seen on the trialling circuit. For speed and ability the Border Collie is clearly designated the superior breed.

She certainly began her 'training' as a sheepdog with certain disadvantages. Not the least of these was an owner whose knowledge and understanding of sheep was zilch and who has only reached a very basic minimum to date with definitely limited prospects of improvement.... and certainly no likelihood of owning her own sheep! Harriet is now 11 years old which makes us both about equal if we apply the 1 dog year being equivalent to 7 human years directive. If we add to that her early lack of access to sheep, I believe it is such an achievement on her behalf to be a working farm dog.

When I found myself floundering with learning the outrun, the lift and the fetch I thought it would be the pinnacle of achievement for me to stand at the post taking part in a sheepdog trial. It felt as though it would be the equivalent of planting my flag on the top of Everest. Things change, I've changed and what I aim for has changed.

It feels so much more to me to watch her doing a job of work, to fetch a large group of sheep in steadily and well... to move them into the pen or down the run with confidence. When she learns a job and does it well and returns as she hears my "that'll do" looking expectant, waiting for me to tell her she's the best farm dog ever.

This is what makes my heart sing now… this is as good as it gets and I say a big thank you to this loyal friend by my side; the one who first took me into this sheepdog world and continues to share her hidden talents with me. 'Tis true they are sometimes well hidden, but even then, more apparent than mine.

When I get the chance to drive Annie's Land Rover myself I begin to feel like a real farmer. Even then I'm needing to learn new skills; I'd never driven an automatic until the first time I attempted to take Annie's car to a different part of the field while she was working with her dogs close at hand and I was moving the transport in readiness for our next task.

* * *

When I was first allocated a car for my district nurse/midwife work I really thought I had reached the highpoint of my career; the job I loved and now a car instead of a bike… a Morris Traveller, who could want more? It's amazing to think back now to that time when with a sticker in the window announcing 'District Nurse on Call', you could park anywhere, even in London; even double park if it was an urgent call. For many years, now district nurses have been prevented from 'advertising' their presence for fear of having our cars broken into for drugs or syringes… changes indeed.

* * *

Now with dogs looking out of each window and maybe a poorly sheep in the back that we're bringing back for extra TLC in a barn on the yard, I feel, even if only for a minute or two, that we're real farm workers Harriet and I. I gained experience parking in the smallest of spaces quickly and easily on the district, I'm now learning how to avoid sheep and ditches. I haven't dared to try reversing with either a trailer or Pratley on the back though.

There are some surprising similarities between district nursing work and sheep farming. Both are somewhat solitary pursuits for much of the time. Out on the district working alone, moving on from one family to the next... on the farm heading around to the next flock of sheep in some far off field. The importance of being able to improvise 'on the job' with whatever equipment is to hand when the need arises is indeed a talent to be valued in both occupations.

* * *

There is no limitless supply of dressings, equipment or maybe even bedlinen in the home. This means that with the uncertainty of what any patient might need as you arrive for a first visit, an innovative approach can be a number one priority.

* * *

What we load into the Land Rover in the yard before setting out on our rounds to the sheep is just as crucial and inventiveness is still often the name of the game. However, finding spare twine to tie a hurdle or two together to make and improvised pen in the corner of a field may be somewhat easier than hastily searching a kitchen for something to use as a bedpan for an immobile bedridden patient. Mind you she was probably less likely to escape than sheep when they manage to totally miss my hastily erected proxy pen, escaping through a hole in the hedge... *(but then as I recall many a patient has also been known to miss my less than perfect substitute bedpan... what a blessing the disposable ones they have now must be.)*

Harriet has got used to bumbling about in the foot-well of Annie's Land Rover as we go up hill and down dale around the sheep fields, some with a gradient too steep to progress straight nose down, where we track across and back till we reach the bottom.

I wave goodbye to Annie as I leave the farm; a treasured friendship. As Harriet lays down on the back seat preparing herself for the drive home, I remind her that she's the lucky one and any other working sheepdog will be in an outside kennel tonight with no promise of marmite crusts for tea, however well he's worked.

All Hail the Judge

I had a great offer today, someone I have great respect for invited me to sit alongside her while she was judging a trial. It was an open trial that was way beyond either mine or Harriet's ability... in fact it will *always* be beyond us I know but it's a great one to watch. If I were ever to find myself partaking in any particular trial, it would be this one, not simply because it's one of the very few trials held in my area of the country but also because Annie and Dan provide the sheep for this one and I have an affection for the sheep Harriet and I have worked and cared for. The course is quite tricky with a long outrun. Harriet and I have worked in this field with a large flock of sheep... it now looks much more exacting when it's set up for a trial.

This year I was able to be with Annie as she chose and moved the selected sheep. So to be offered the opportunity to learn about some of the mysteries of judging adds an extra dimension to the day for me.

Harriet does not join in with my enthusiasm and does what she usual does when we're at a trial and she's not being invited to take part. She at first looks distinctly bored with the whole procedure, throws me a look of disgust at not ensuring her a turn and very quickly retires to sleep on the back seat of the judge's car.

As soon as I started learning about sheepherding and the sport of trialling, how the points are allocated for the various stages of the trial course filter through from all sides. Particularly at the big national and international, trials I found myself listening to all the experienced voices around me as I sat either in the stands or in the midst of the gaggle of spectators gathering along the fence with the best all round view of the course...

"Oh I'd definitely have taken a couple off that outrun, it wasn't a good shape to my mind" "Well I've never liked a dog who sets off for the fence like that, he'll lose a lot for that!"

"Lovely steady lift there, must have got full marks for that... bloody good dog that one; always said he'd do well!"

All this around me while I'm thinking, "What was wrong with that ... looked good to me!" I understood how many marks were allotted for each element but really had only a vague notion of how good was good and what was very good. After all if the only trials you've taken part in you've had to give up and retire, you never get to see what marks were allotted for the bits of the course you did complete; you just receive a large R next to yours and the dog's name on the mark sheet. Harriet and I have quite a large collection of different shaped Rs recorded by many a fluent hand but sadly a substantial number of Rs doesn't equal a rosette of any colour. The few trials I have participated in where I have not needed to retire maybe very few, but when the clock has beaten us and we've run out of time, it was helpful because then points already gained are maintained enabling me to assess how many points I had gained for the parts of the trial we had managed to complete.

I remember being surprised that there was no actual training course to be become a judge and that while the total marks allotted to each element of the trial seemed mandatory, there were considerable differences between how each judge would allocate marks or penalise certain transgressions. Talking to one judge she admitted to deducting at least half the outrun points for any dog who ran out to the fence as a starting point... whereas I've known others who don't feel so strongly that this is necessarily 'incorrect', particularly for the working farm dog.

Other judges would accept what might seem to be a doubtful shed, believing the dog must display more evidently that it is not merely coming through to split off the two sheep, but is holding them, preventing them re-joining the others.

I think I've learned that what is really essential in any given judging session is fairness throughout that trial. No-one seems to complain about either generous or harsh marking as long as it is impartial and even-handed. I'm also struck by just how concentrated the judging process is. There is very little time between one run and the next. Literally there is only the time taken to get the sheep off the course and into the 'exhaust pen' at one end plus the time to allow those 'letting out' to assemble the next five at the top of the field.

Now the judge will be lucky if it's Harriet they're marking on the run since, should we manage to complete the course and I reopen the pen gate at the finish to a round of clapping, she insists on holding them in the pen, steadfastly refusing to let them out ever again!

There is no time to avert eyes during any run. Focus has to be continual to pick up any possible contravention or wrongdoing such as 'gripping' and assessing the merits of dog plus handler constantly. Gripping is when the dog bites the sheep and it is only acceptable in exceptional circumstances on the trial field and would normally mean you're disqualified and if you don't automatically decide to leave the field, the judge would ask you to do so. The very occasional exceptional circumstances would be if the sheep 'stood' to the dog, and refused to turn off when the dog has moved steadily forward and is face to face with the sheep. In this case a quick bite on the nose where the dog immediately let's go maybe tolerated if it is considered the dog had no other option. If the dog grabs and snatches wool or hangs on to a sheep as it tries to turn, the run is immediately over. In farm work too, the dog is only allowed to grip under circumstances when the sheep is challenging the dog's authority. Some dogs when they are learning the herding craft have to be taught it's not acceptable to grip. It's not a problem I've had to overcome with Harriet; she has always been able to exert her influence over 'stroppy' sheep by showing her teeth in a fierce looking grimace which I gather is an unusual tactic to make the sheep behave.

This was such an opportunity for me today, more learning to build on, more notes to make when I get home. As I drive away from the trial I'm thinking about how the sheep Harriet and I try to work now would judge us? When we move them, take them through gates, pen them and guide through the footbath... how they would judge the quality of our craftsmanship?

I know when the judge adjudicates our efforts on the field, there is only an allocated mark. No comments are given such as 'attention to detail required when penning' or 'outrun beginning to improve'. Maybe to administer a mark without remarks has its advantages. Any school-like report mark sheet with a comments column would undoubtedly in our case, detail too many transgressions; 'considerable room for improvement' might be at the top of the list or 'unlikely to obtain a high grade' or 'shows little promise at this time'... rather reminiscent of any report I've ever received on anything.

However, I lift my spirits as I think that if the sheep on the farm were asked for feedback they may just say "well that raggy dog is slowly getting better, she seems to know a bit more about what she's supposed to be doing, and can at least tell her right from her left now, not sure the owner can though".

If it wasn't for encouragement from Annie, I know we'd have fallen by the wayside in our struggles long ago. She constantly points out what Harriet can manage this week that she couldn't before or talks about how far she has come saying "Do you remember when she wouldn't even go all the way up that hill, let alone bring all those sheep down?" Annie 'judging' our competence on the farm work is so much more meaningful to me.

I think I started this sheep dog stuff with Harriet believing it was all about using her instincts to maximise her quality of life. Following on from this, it seemed aiming to trial with her was the way to go; and now it's allowing her to use any skills she might possibly develop to take on a life pretending we're a part-time farmer and working sheep dog. Who would ever have guessed that this is where I would find myself?

Indeed, who would have guessed what happened next. The clinics continued to be important in our life together for both myself and Harriet or, using Annie's nickname for her, for Lady H and I. I wondered at times if I should feel a bit of an imposter now in the clinic because I knew that I wasn't here really practising with aspirations of striding to the post at the next trialling season. But I was able to bring back everything I learned at each clinic and practise those and improve each and every manoeuvre I attempted on the farm.

My ambition had moved on or, some might say, had gone backwards. We both so enjoyed the farm work, I wanted to have a dog who competently worked the sheep on the farm. Where I could know that we are able to carry out tasks well and unaided, where we were a useful pair for Annie to have around and where she didn't have to send Joey (her top dog) to rescue us and the sheep, on too many occasions. Way back when we started the clinics I would certainly not have guessed how our objectives would have changed. Did I have a right to be here now when the other dogs present were already doing farm work but were now aiming at something higher, some greater peak on which to plant their flag?

And yet today, while I don't actually have an answer as to whether or not I have the right to be here, I do know it's been a day I'll not forget in a hurry. A cold, windy, rainy day that no-one would believe could deliver anything worth cherishing and yet I'm so bubbling with excitement that I don't care about the whys and wherefores of anything. I've just finished my last training session of this clinic and, I just want to 'throw my hat' in the air except that it's not *a* hat, it's 3 hats; a jerkin attached one, a woolly knitted one and a rain hat with a peak. I'm risking losing my boots in the mud with every step as I wade towards the gate

I'm laughing as I remember the last occasion when I threw my hat in the air. It was my mortar board when I passed my masters degree... a somewhat more auspicious occasion perhaps than this event. However this happening was about to become equally exhilarating, in fact earth-shattering...

My glasses are misted-up, and Harriet looks like a pitiful spectacle as she returns to my side and we prepare to leave the field. I was pleased with how it had gone, over-joyed with how she'd worked throughout with challenging sheep, particularly when we shed two of the five and she confidently drove them off down the field, looking for all the world as though she was partaking in the championship.

As a dishevelled looking pair we approach our trainer who has not taken his eyes off us throughout. I hesitate, waiting for his response... how did he feel we'd done, what was he going to say? I must remember what he says I need to improve before returning to the next clinic...

The words rang out and are still resounding in my ears, (but then I did ask him to repeat it in case I'd misheard!)

"Well that was an *excellent* session from both of you"!

This was a word that I had never heard him use and had it ever been uttered it had certainly not come in our direction.

Perhaps after all we were making progress, perhaps after everything that had gone before, it was possible for us to grasp this game we're playing... this extraordinary art-form I'd become addicted to.

As I meet the other group members advancing for their turns I jump up and down like a five year old and toss my crook in the air as I share my excitement and they all join in, sharing my delight.

Life doesn't get much better than this... who needs a rosette?!

How Sweet is the Shepherd's Sweet Lot

(William Blake)

When I'm heading towards perhaps the concluding chapters of my life, this unexpected happening that I might have considered impossible as I journeyed into retirement has enriched both our lives. Here's hoping that we both have many more pages in our lifespan journal left to write on.

There is something about the writing of a book that in some ways mimics retirement. Most of us come into retirement not quite sure where we're going and certainly when I began writing, I wasn't sure where it would take me. Maybe, when we're uncertain about what might lie ahead, looking back gives us confidence. Perhaps simply turning over past events of head and heart helps make sense of where we've been, which might allow us to stride forward rather than stay as we are now, waiting for something to happen.

* * *

As I entered retirement I was saddened by the changes happening in the career I had left behind; I had spent almost all my working life district nursing, believing the science and art of nursing were delivered at its best in patients' homes.

Instead of allowing our district nurses to develop this highly valued art of home nursing, it had now become a career where nursing protégés are being taught to serve management rather than patients, where quality is pushed aside, buried under an ever increasing pile of tasks.

* * *

In many ways, I welcomed retirement. Many would say it is the beginning of the end. While it is clearly a marker leading us on into old age, it could also be said that really all it does is announce the end of one life and beginning of another. A more accurate and certainly a more appealing proclamation of where we're heading might be "What comes next?" rather than simply trying just to adjust to growing old.

As I stumble on some uneven rabbit-hole-ridden banks on the farm, I'm reminded of how fortunate I have been to be in good enough health to take advantage of what accidentally came next when I left my career.

The fitness of patients had always been a much greater priority in my life than my own and the words of the matron in my training hospital sometimes comes back to haunt me.

"You are rich in health and strength and everything the ill need... training as a nurse is about giving that goodness to all of those you care for"

I suspect many of us as student nurses reflected on those words many times at the end of a twelve hour night shift when we felt any health and strength we may once have had was long gone. Quaint and fanciful as those words now sound, it comes from a time when nursing was seen as a vocation, a career of 'service' to which you *gave* of yourself... not quite 'carrying a lamp' but almost.

But then Harriet the rescue puppy arrived with her own demands... needing to be walked and walked and walked some more. Any fitness I have managed to gather on this journey towards continually getting older (with knees that definitely feel older than my years), are due to her.

* * *

Come to think of it, matron was right, the 'health and strength' of my knees has certainly been given to lifting all those patients up the bed by climbing up into the middle of a very dipped, sagging double mattress, positioning myself behind the patient and manoeuvring many a heavy prone immobile body up to a sitting position at the head of the bed taking the strain through my legs rather than my back; all before the Moving and Handling, Health and Safety Manual was invented!

* * *

But then Harriet the rescue puppy arrived with her own demands. Her need for walks has certainly been instrumental in any fitness level I've managed to maybe just about hold on to... not that it's anything to shout about, but it does relieve me of any guilt about not going to the gym; but then perhaps if I had been preoccupied with head bands and leg warmers and joined the gym gang I would now be able to swing my legs over five barred gates with ease. I have heard that the gym is the 'in' place to go to meet future partners these days; either that or 'on-line' I understand.

How glad am I to be released from the need or want to go looking for a mate ... good job since both my computer and athletic skills are decidedly limited. I feel fortunate to have arrived at this stage of my life enjoying living alone... well no-one living with a dog to whom they're devoted can truthfully say they live alone.

Many times through my career I reflected on how great it was to be working in a job that made me happy. We spend a large percentage of our lives earning a living. If each working day is nothing more than drudgery, an existence you're simply doing to earn money, waiting to escape before you can be happy, how long those days must be.

And here I am now, still happy. The top of that list of happiness is here in front of me now as we walk together over the common. When you have a 'partner' who wags a tail when she sees you, who is so evidently pleased when you're around, there is no way you can escape joining in with gladness and belief that all is right with your world! Maybe it is she who has enabled me to choose the single life... to be truly happy living alone. Some might say it's a quiet life living alone. I'm not sure I'd agree.

I think it was Bertrand Russell who said:

"A happy life must be to a great extent a quiet life, for it
is only in an atmosphere of quiet that true joy dare live".

Something in there resonates with me, it maybe that when 'quiet' translates as 'lonely' that living alone comes to be seen unhappy and less joyful. I find myself in a new phase of life... a life I cherish, an unexpected life of fun and enthusiasm, working the sheep on the farm with Harriet, ever mindful of living in the moment. I do recognise that I have less life ahead of me than behind me and, like so many of us as we grow older, I notice with regret the increased wrinkles, the boobs that don't seem to support themselves anymore and of course the arthritic knees that refuse to work as they did.

I, probably more than most, and more evidently than many, know how life can change in the blink of an eye and yet I admit to giving very little of my time contemplating the 'what ifs...' of my future.

But maybe all of these physical declines are not the worst possible fate we are presented with; maybe saying goodbye to things we have a passion for, precious conversations with loved ones, early morning bird song... anything we hold dear that enflames our enthusiasm, maybe these are the losses we fear most as we grow older... and maybe the prospect of these forfeitures is sufficiently bleak that our mind retreats from concentrating on such an inevitability. It is therefore the impossibility of performance that prevents us anticipating or envisaging such losses.

Somehow, I'm discovering that as we grow old, and as our physical body rusts, we are rewarded with a deeper level of something that it's hard to find words for. Maybe it's a contentment with who we are, or perhaps an independence of thought that requires no commendation but somehow overcomes other limitations. Possibly we simply learn as we age to engage fully with all we have.

* * *

I remember a kindly man I had nursed for a long time, who, when he had only days to live, sharing with me how he appreciated things more deeply now. He described the tree he could see from his window, explaining what it meant to him. "It's always been beautiful" he said, "but this year the blossom is stunning, it's the blossomiest blossom ever" Was this because he believed he wouldn't see it again or maybe the sight surfaced and touched senses never previously exposed?

* * *

Perhaps only as we age do we begin to understand the depth, the fundamental reality which we have lived and maybe it is growing older that offers us the time and mental space to do so... hopefully while still allowing us to look forward to all that has yet to be discovered.

It seems both head and heart come together with meaning that takes us to our own inimitable place of joy that surmounts all else... well almost; I'm still desirous of long legs that I could swing easily over a five barred farm gate!

I have a plaque hung on my wall that declares:

This is the season for fine wine, roses and drunken friends
Enjoy this moment
This moment is your life.

As I look at it now, with Harriet's head on my lap, I reconfigure the inscription to read:

This is the season for shepherding with Harriet
Enjoy this moment
This moment is my life

... my heart sings.

The End

Glossary

I'm not claiming the absolute accuracy of meaning for any of the terms stated here. Many seem to have slightly different interpretations in each different book I've read and often between many of the sheepdog trainers I've spoken to. This is in no way a definitive list.

Aaway Command given to send dog round sheep to the right

Broken mouthed A sheep losing its teeth

Come-bye Command given to send dog round sheep to the left

Cast When a sheep is lying on its back unable to get up

Draft A ewe not going to tup anymore, usually moved to lower ground (may sometimes referred to as 'cast' ewe)

Ewe A female sheep

Fat lambs Lambs being raised to be sold for meat

Flanking The movements a dog makes as he runs around the sheep

Flock A group of sheep

Gimmer A young sheep in her second year usually when being kept for breeding

Grip When a dog grabs at a sheep

Heft The area on an open hill that sheep know they belong to.

Hogg A young sheep that has been fully weaned, usually those destined for slaughter

In Lamb A pregnant ewe

Lamb A young sheep in its first year

Lift The first point of contact the dog makes with the sheep

Pen An enclosure to hold livestock

Race A narrow fenced area that only allows the sheep to move in single file

Ringing The application of rubber rings for male castration and tail docking

Ram A male sheep

Square flank An exaggerated flank

Shedding The act of separating off one or more sheep from the pack

Sheepdog trial A competitive sport which requires the handler to command his sheepdog to perform a variety of challenges that mimic various working tasks

Tup A ram/male sheep

Wether A castrated male sheep

Acknowledgments

Annie has to be at the top of my list of thanks. To offer Harriet and I access to her sheep way back then when we were both still at the beginning of our struggles, with little more to recommend us than our enthusiasm, was an opportunity that I had absolutely no right to expect. Yet it has been the single entity that has contributed the most to any progress that Harriet and I have started to make on the shepherding front. But it has given me so much more; it has so enriched my life, giving me a retirement I could only ever have dreamt about and a chance to share a working relationship with my dog. Your friendship Annie is a precious one.

Jed Watson for teaching me about Beardies and tolerating me so patiently at the clinics when it takes me so long to learn anything at all; and not giving up on me when I get it wrong…again! For answering all those questions I keep asking. Giving up so much of his time at these very special clinics that have added another dimension to my life.

Thank you Elaine for all the work organising these clinics and Susie for your continued encouragement each time I attend and those ever-helpful videos!

Charles Bowden in his book The Last Shepherds for interesting me in the history of farming

To Dave Thompson for all his encouragement and giving his sheep and fields to many of us who are early learners in the sheep trialling game plus all those family members who set up and run the trials there… and parsnip and honey soup to die for!

To all the many sheepdog triallers and their books that have inspired and encouraged me along the way.

Also, not to be forgotten, thanks to friends and family for all the encouragement, and proof reading... not least my very special writing friends; those monthly luncheons have been a lifesaver, with all the exceedingly honest feedback while convincing me I really did have something worth saying.

Printed in Poland
by Amazon Fulfillment
Poland Sp. z o.o., Wrocław

62239342R00081